T0316619

BOTSOTSO 16

Contemporary South African Culture

Published by

Botsotso Publishing
Box 30952
Braamfontein
2017

botsotso@artslink.co.za
www.botsotsoportal.co.za

ISBN 978-0-9814205-2-3

We thank the Multi Agency Grants Initiative for its funding support.

Multi Agency Grants Initiative

Cover, text design and layout:
Advance Graphics

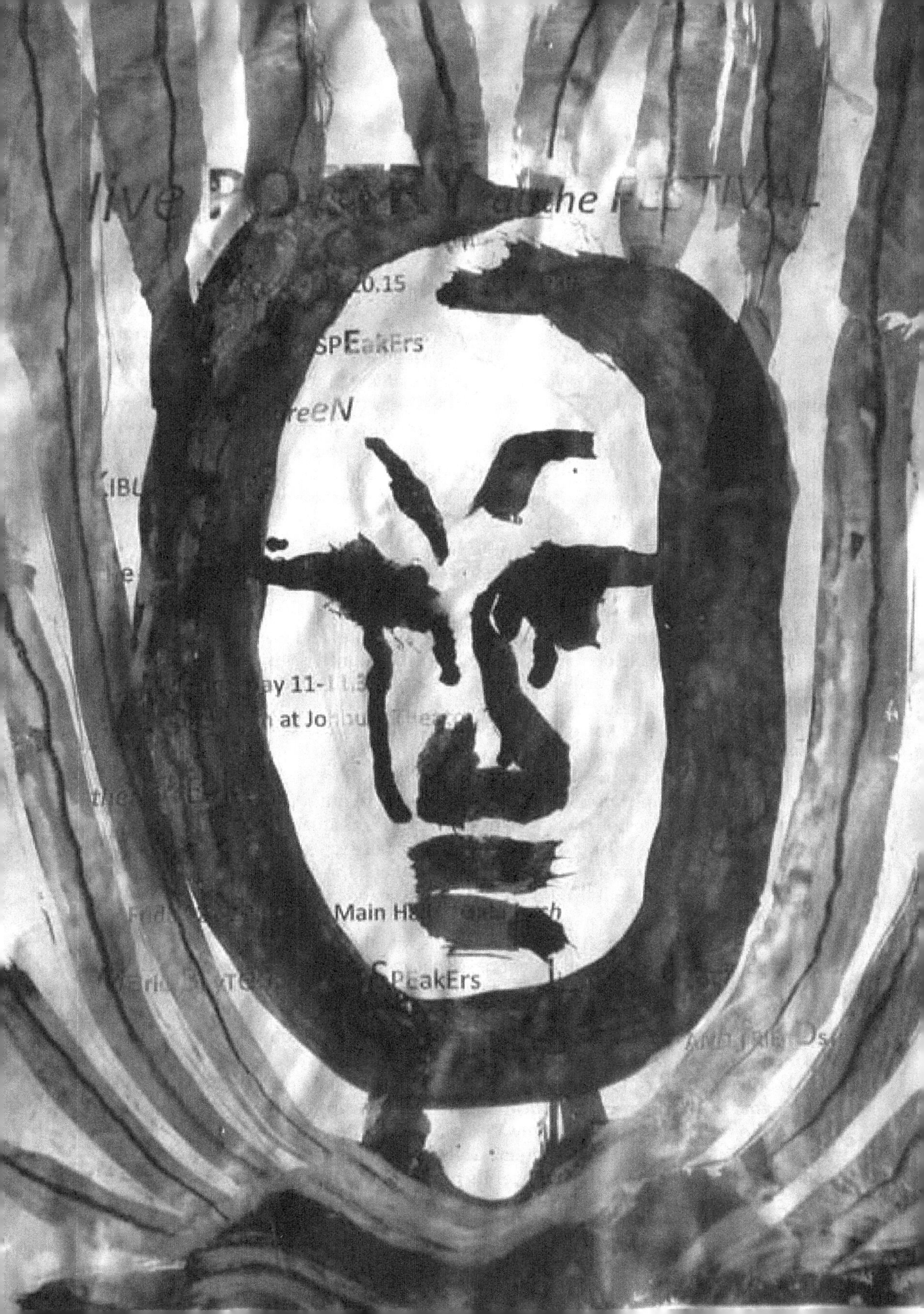

EDITORIAL

Yes, Botsotso in 'hard cover' is back! For the past three years, due to a lack of funds, we have had to restrict publishing to the website (now at www.botsotsoportal.co.za). In this regard much thanks to Deon-Simphiwe Skade for keeping the website active, both as co-editor and as webmaster, and to the Multi Agency Grants Initiative for providing sufficient funds to cover the publication of two hard cover journals.

Having started with the 'good news' is there more to come? – considering that the past three years have seen a number of 'problematics' worsen. For is it not true to say that we are living through a dry season as far as culture is concerned? Is the vitality of our society not ebbing away in terms of general interest in the 'serious' arts (as opposed to entertainment and sporting diversions) – particularly with respect to literature and theatre that tackle the root issues defining our lives? Has the promise of radical change (which would include financial support for creative projects in all the arts) been stifled by incompetency and corruption? A key example is the misuse of the National Lottery Development Trust Fund (NLTDF). We also know that the Department of Arts and Culture (DAC) funding for literature has been reduced and that its annual calls for funding applications have been cut back (from two to one); literacy levels are floundering (as evidenced by recent literacy and numeracy tests of our schools pupils); sales of books by the chain stores and independents have fallen as the overall economic recession has caused purchasing power to drop and steep increases in printing prices have raised book prices by more than 30% over the past two years. South Africa's Internet penetration is still below 15% of the population. As such, both e-book sales and e-sales of hard cover books are too low to make up for the drop in over-the-counter sales. To sum up: there appears to be both a crisis with respect to interest in 'serious' art making and in its economic base with the result that the Printed Word, and everything associated with it – intellectual vigour, promotion of in-depth debate and enquiry – seem to be on a down slide. So does this mean that literary life is dying in South Africa?

The answer on the creative side is absolutely not. And just one proof is the vitality and quality of the poems, stories, essays and art work brought together in this edition. This quality is reflected in both the range of the themes and situations dealt with and in their depth and vital use of language. So we are not at all despondent about the actual work being produced by an increasing number of writers. **The concern arises from the means available to keep publishing and then the means to distribute such work as widely as possible.**

For some time now Botsotso has tried to engage with the National Library system and with the National Arts Council (in collaboration with a number of NGO's in the cultural field) to secure funding for the sort of inclusive, contemporary literature that we are trying to promote – literature that the mainstream publishers will generally not touch.

The model put forward is quite simple: **That the National Arts Council (NAC) provide seed money for several publications; that the national library system then buy a copy of each of these publications for the over 3,000 public libraries spread out over the country; that the Department of Education also buy one copy for every school library (despite the terrible statistic that only 15% of schools currently have libraries there are still several thousand such libraries). Given these numbers, a print run of 6,000 copies of each of these books will cover its production and leave a sizeable surplus which can be ploughed back into new publications. In this way the publisher will** never again have to receive funding from another source and, as importantly, will (potentially) reach hundreds of thousands of both adults and children. Of course, the quality of the publications will have to be monitored but that is in any case the function of the NAC's literature committee – we are talking here not of censorship but of maintaining an objectively high level of literary expression.

Despite several meetings with representatives of the DAC, the national library system and the NAC, no progress has been made – in fact, despite vague indications that the idea was seen as worth pursuing no concrete response has been received from these key state departments. As such, projects like Botsotso will continue to stutter on and hope that other funding agencies that are more proactive and concerned about 'non-commercial' writing will step into the breach.

Having said this, there are indications that the tide may be turning. Indeed, we had very good news a few weeks ago. **A determined coalition of non-profit organizations has forced the Department of Trade and Industry (under whose jurisdiction the NLDTF falls) to adopt several very important recommendations that will bring the NLDTF under far greater public scrutiny and control and thus enhance its effectiveness.** We can only hope that these very welcome and long overdue changes will bear fruit because the future of many important and worthwhile organizations and projects is dependent on the support they can and should get from the NLTDF. Witnessing (and to an extent, participating) in this campaign was very encouraging and goes to prove (yet again) **that without effective organization such necessary changes will not come about.**

Indeed, the central problem still facing the development of a national literature that embraces all our society's varied cultures, languages and experiences is **the lack of a writer's organization with a non-profit publishing house that distributes the work being produced outside of the commercial realm.** The collapse of Cosaw and Cosaw Publishing and the passing of Staffrider in the 1990s were setbacks that we have still to recover from. Journals like Botsotso have attempted to fill this vacuum but the absence of a writers organizations with chapters around the country has meant that distribution of literary journals is haphazard and uneven and that the advancement of literature and literacy cannot take place in a systematic way and so reach the multitudes of people who live outside of the world of books.

The rebuilding of a writers organization is thus a central task. But is there any sign that the DAC and the NAC are alive to this? Sadly, the answer is no. Inertia and indifference seem to rule. How can we wake them up? Bua, maqabane, bua! And write about it, 'perform about it' and then (like the coalition formed to challenge the NLTDF), let's toyi-toyi so that they get the message and start taking their mandate to serve South African culture seriously.

Allan Kolski Horwitz   Mboneni Ike Muila   Siphiwe ka Ngwenya

CONTENTS

Pages remote
by Mike Alfred

Does anyone anticipate the journal's next issue?
Anyone apart from him/herself, that is?
Is anyone disappointed by a poet's absence?
Does she/he have a favourite?
Does his/her heart react on reading him/her?
Does she/he sigh, shed a tear? Does the poet work on him/her?
Is there anyone who values this poet as a source of inspiration,
of enjoyment, of instruction?
Does anyone study the style, the word play, the philosophy?
Hey, steady on, don't let's get carried away!
Would this poet ever know he/she's appreciated or dismissed?
Is the poet used in class? Is she/he recited on the radio?
Poor bugger lives in a vast bowl of silence.
How dare he/she expect some recognition?
Would any reader be boldly tempted to converse with poets?
Might poets be tempted to converse with other poets?
Are we literary lepers? Are we of another galaxy?
Are we not to be taken seriously, dismissed like pesky kids?
Are we half a sip in the ocean of life?
Poetry writing is surely the most remote, lonely art form.
On reflection, does the poet choose the medium for its suffering?
Is the poet shy and introverted, eccentric, half balmy perhaps,
Not tough enough to take the knocks?
Is poetry itself a literary wasteland, a fetid backwater?
Is poetry in unliterary SA, a huge joke, a curiosity?
Something ugly and deformed in a side-show tent?
Have we entered a world where we're on a hiding to nothing?

Who's that waiting for the next issue?

A Story Of More Woe
by Vanita Nyembezi Phiri

The teacher's muddy legs were shaking-shaking because he grew impatient with Hope, and restless with the rapid speed at which Pain progressed. The shirt he wore was pricked with burrs of weeds and hardened in places by dry blood. The boy sitting next to him had offered a slumber jacket but the teacher refused. He kept apologising, thanking and panting because he feared that he had placed the boy's life at risk.

"It's almost sunrise," the boy said.

The teacher and the boy sat on top of wizened maize in a granary that stood elevated from the ground. Their buttocks should have ached but their vagrant minds were too far away to feel anything.

"I'm sure your wife is okay, sir," assured the boy. He was about fifteen and he barely said anything in class – if he came at all. But on that night that everything, including stars, shined and winked to betray, there he was trying to utter words that meant so much.

"Let us pray so." The teacher's voice was croaky.

The teacher was aware that as much as he feared for the boy's life, his own was in graver danger. The boy's parents could blow the whistle on him by calling on the cruel and callous mob that was dancing around the streets with axes and guns.

As if the boy had read the teacher's mind, he said, "You are safe here. My father is a good man. Besides, aren't you a Hutu, sir?"

"I am. But my wife, as you know, is not. And so they will kill us both". The teacher raised his head as if to observe the converging dry grass and reeds that made up the thatched roof.

"Well, my father will not have you or your wife killed. He's not involved in this conflict."

The teacher had met the boy's father in his early days of the posting. He was content back then, full of fresh ideas for himself and his class. But his mind could not seek too much comfort in the placid past. The popping sound of AK-47s brought him back to the here-and-now. He imagined the ensuing chaos at the nearby village. A few hours ago he had been there where he once called home; there where the peace of the night had been tainted with streaks, spatters, spills and gushes of bloody red. This made him think, re-think and un-think the horrid ways his wife could meet her end.

"I can get you some guavas from the tree outside, sir," said the boy. The teacher declined.

The boys' parents were unaware of the presence of a fugitive English teacher in their granary. The teacher had asked that the boy keep the matter to himself. "Until I can think of something," he said.

"Where do you plan to go, sir?"

He wiped his tears and, in a flash, felt the nothingness that prevailed. "To fetch my wife and flee." He paused and added, "If we can."

He had left his wife hiding at some unmentionable place where even fresh air was reluctant to flow. Her physicality, which had charmed many, had become her defect: her height and skin were as Tutsi as they came.

"Why do you show little interest in my class?" When the teacher posed the question, he was less interested in the answer and more in talking for the sake of preserving his sanity.

On normal days, teachers asked their students such questions. On normal days, students did anything to avoid such questions. But these were not normal days and the boy had never been so unsparing. "I find literature difficult, sir."

"Can you be more specific?"

"Well…er…Shakespeare." He felt self-indulgent to whine about such triviality. "It's the language, the stories plus I cannot relate to the characters." The teacher looked weak and the boy could sense that even listening required much effort. "To be honest," the boy continued, "I think Romeo and Juliet is a stupid story. I don't see any African boy behaving like Romeo". He tried to explain himself before a series of bangs and shrieks not too far away interrupted him.

They held their words for a while. Then the teacher said, "Go on."

"I mean I prefer stories about African people."

"So it is resonance you seek?"

"Resonance: I like that word. Yes, resonance, sir"

"What do you think Romeo and Juliet is about?"

He wanted to impress his teacher with a good answer. He thought hard before he spat what he considered obvious. "Love." Then he offered a controlled chuckle. "Though Romeo and Juliet's love is not powerful enough to save them."

"Shh!" The teacher thought he had heard some footsteps but the boy assured him that no one was awake. They waited in silence while the boy quietly stood up and peeked outside."

"It's a dog, sir. The neighbour's dog sniffing around."

They waited for a little while. Then they heard a cock-a-doodle-doo announcing a dead world coming to life. By this time, the gunshots had stopped.

"Have you ever been in love or seen anyone in love?" The teacher later asked.

"Yes, I think so."

"And hatred?"

"Yes."

"Well in that case you have more in common with Romeo that you realise. Do you think your conception of Love and Hate is any different to that of sixteenth century Verona?" Some light was penetrating into the granary and the teacher knew that he would soon have to release the boy.

"I think I understand what you're saying," the boy wanted to continue but his sentence was leading him back to that dark place where they were trying so hard to escape. He held back his words but the teacher gave him a prompting look.

"You do?"

The boy nodded. "It's like your story, sir. You and your wife are like Romeo and Juliet – the Tutsis and the Hutus are The Capulets and Montagues"

"First you look down on Romeo. And now you liken me to him. Shall I take it as a compliment?" He said these words with a kind of sad smile while the boy glanced at him with animated eyes.

"No, sir…I mean yes. You and your wife cannot be together because you belong to feuding tribes."

"So you believe the overarching theme to be Hate?"

"Um, yes. But Hate is related to Love."

"But it is not Love."

"So the play is about both Love and Hate then?"

"For years Romeo and Juliet's families have feuded."

Here the boy used his hands to show his frustration. "And the play doesn't even explain why."

"Perhaps the reason behind the feud is not as crucial. Let me ask you something: what happens once Romeo and Juliet die?"

"Well, their families make up."

"Indeed. So what you are saying is that the play is not a tragedy."

"But people die so it is still a tragedy."

They heard voices – at first they were uncertain whether it was of Hope or Despair. The teacher glanced at the boy and immediately knew how their story would unfold. The boy, no longer looking him in the eye, shed a tear, then two.

There was a bang, and then they were ordered to come down.

Unspeakable things happened to the teacher – or they did not. It does not matter anymore because the teacher and the boy were minor characters of a long story. Three whole months passed of widowing, maiming, dismembering and cries so loud they could have awoken the one million massacred bodies.

Years later, after people had forgotten the teacher and the boy had grown into a man, the story continued. It continues to this day in the streets of Murumbi, Kigali, Kinshasa, Cairo, Soweto, across the seas and in our heads.

TWO POEMS
by Frank Meintjies

Madiba's pistol

a rusted
artefact
or: potent symbol
– some distance
from the compost heap
where the tiniest bits
of green
sprout
its trigger
cool as nails
(or as chilled words)
caressed by slithering worms

in the corner
a kind of centrepiece
a magnetic
tree
shading
a small area

just a house
a relic
– suburban flagship
of
so many meetings
so many bolt-holes
in so many
places
so many
nocturnal
rendezvous

a house
strangely seeded,
turned
'intriguing'
by an old gun

the soothsayer
(cutely lying)
says madiba's gun
remains cocked

for the pan africanist
this item's
the incendiary seed
from which
the new revolution
will rise

the capitalists
ever looking
for safe havens
want to know
how much
it's worth
– they scan
the near horizon
of
the auctioneer's
pages

amnesia, alzheimer's & the old poet

black poet-intellectual, scribe
scribbler
at times markedly ordinary in feelings
in that dishevelledness
plain as spilt (or split) grape
in the crate's bottom

mostly out of season

in brutal & painful times
brunt-bearing & vulnerable
often condemned as addicted to recklessness

now, in times of rebuilding
washed sidesetream

the young who don't know
your fierce testimonies
too tender to remember
how you thrived
brandishing bravado like a fist, like a small gun

the young
we love them, their minds
flooded by channels, images, holograms
& slick aspirations
but you, you don't fit
they laugh their derision
snigger as your argument forms
as old words roll off a jaded tongue
they laugh
at your void-of-style
dress and cut

they ask: are you for real?

how can they know that
your okapi's nib
now broken off in places
carved rough words on street corners

life is like the wind
like the existence of dreams
like your wan smile
as you peer into handwritten pages

as you trace
on the back of your hand
the overgrown foliage
of lines and veins

not you too
forgotten
how those rough-hewn hands lobbed bruised words
that wander the streets
how your sharp instrument
dug footholds and handles
in unsteady & precarious times

TWO POEMS

by Brian Walter

Slip

In memoriam Jaya Ruthnam

We could happily slip the fence
through our shared gate
to borrow a cup of chillies
from the best of neighbours,
and a beard-shaking laugh basela,
till the cup ran over:
do you remember that Diwali,
with your path of garden candles
and our children running circles
in your night yard, quick sparklers flying?
Yet there was always more
we sought, always the feeling
that we'd like to get closer
to the breathing being of you,
always the promise,
and promised yoga to do,
except time slips away,
slips, as the puff-adder
once into your garden, and you
frantic for children and dogs
— your concern always with others:
the jar of sweets you kept always
full for any kid who'd slip softly by;
funds you'd source to help the young to college
against the rising tides of poverty;
our strike for workers' rights
you led with your essence of care and sense
of light:
which was the very breath of you,
and the breath was all,
you'd tell us quietly,
sitting cross-legged, upon our bottom bones:
all.
As we breathe now,
holding it,
remembering, you, now
your breath
has slipped
through the gate,
back into your light of garden.

Otherwise

Since Christ was born
– his parents travelling for a census –
and died, rendering his body to Caesar,
his soul to sacrifice,
we have learned to be counted
and politically defined:
that Christian beginning looking
to the sextriple mark of the Revelation:
thus they come this year,
forms in hand, now the post-apartheid
people, who still ask my mixed up
kids to define officially their own race
for their forms and statistics,
rationalizing race-thinking, confusing the kids
marking them in their own, and everyone's
consciousness – these Caesar-evil
ways of governance. Thus,
when the census guy comes,
let into our house by a son
darker than the enumerator himself,
and sits with me, lighter now than he,
and asks our family's race,
I say – and how else – that I don't know:
"Is this family black, white, asian or coloured?"
I don't know: none of those, or
perhaps some of some, all mixed
in our family. So he smiles, and offers
"Other" as a category suitable for us,
and I take it. We are other,
officially now, and counted. Some will
still treat me as they see me,
and activate their own prejudices,
but let me be other: my place of residence
and occupation, I'll render to Caesar,
what's left I'll render to myself,
the mystery of God, and being otherwise.

Stofo

by Hlengiwe Mnguni

There is a man on the 5 o'clock train from Pretoria to Johannesburg. He is blind. He walks led by a bored teenage boy from coach to coach. He sings and plucks playful notes from the strings of his shiny plum guitar. His songs are witty, sometimes naughty, always lively and fun.

The commuters love him and they always toss more coins into a cup the boy holds to make the couple stay longer before moving on to the next coach.

"Stofo!" they call out, with coins in hand. "Mina ng'fun' iGifted!"

Everyone is already laughing in anticipation of the song whose words change as and when the singer sees fit, but always about twisted divine gifts and talent: Other people are gifted in witchcraft, other people have been blessed with sloth, others are talented at promiscuity - even that is a gift - other people are skilled in the art of making people part with their money. Everything is a gift, good or bad. "Wonk'umunt'unesipho sakhe," declares Stofo.

The 5 o'clock crowd roars with laughter. The boy uninterestedly holds out the cup to the outstretched hands with coins dangling on finger tips. He doesn't smile, like Stofo. With one hand he holds the cup, with the other he methodically helps steer the guitar past the thin shiny poles that run down the centre and the standing bodies. He keeps perfect balance and holds out the blue plastic cup.

They disappear weaving through the crowd, the sound of music and the accompanying laughter still loud but fading. It leaves behind a chaos of conversation about relationships, money, stories of old women caught wide-eyed and naked at three in the morning in a neighbour's yard.

The door at the other end of the coach opens and closes. The music and laughter is gone, and leaves behind a vacuum which everyone quite suddenly starts filling with stories about pain and struggle, familiar everyday stories that make up each of their lives.

One man is up at three in the morning and is only back home at eight in the evening, five days a week. Friday is pay day. Sometimes he drinks half his pay and only comes back the next morning to a disappointed wife, hung over and ashamed. He would like to stop, "but how?" he asks to no one in particular.

Someone earnestly recommends Jesus. Conversation dies down and a vendor walks past quietly. The Christian buys a pack of cards and begins to assemble a group of regular players. The young ones pull out small packages wrapped in brown paper from the insides of their jackets. A woman stares distastefully as one of them, in regulation overalls, empties out the green contents onto the heavily made-up face of a soap actress who decorates the front page of a Sunday tabloid; the actress has split from her husband and the nation deserves, must (!) know.

Soon there is a pungent cloud of dreams in the coach. The people play while the youngsters smoke. They play, they smoke; they think how the world has gone to the dogs. Stofo goes in and out of the coaches, one after the other, while the boy opens and closes the door for him, guiding him through the crowded train as he sings praises to the bountiful gifts that fate has bestowed upon humanity.

Somewhere Between Isando and Germiston the train comes to a slow stop. There is an almost identical look on the faces in the coach. They all will the train not to stop. Each person wills it to continue chugging along the tracks at least until "I get to Germiston" or "Park Station". But it stops. For an hour and a half during which little is said the train stands idle as the sun sets.

There are a few guesses at the cause of the inconvenient stop: perhaps the train has hit someone; perhaps it is avoiding a collision up ahead. People will miss their connections; they will get to taxi ranks to find only sprawling empty spaces. They are worried and quiet. Nothing happens, and nobody sets the train on fire like other passengers on other trains in similar situations have done and ended up on the seven o'clock news. Nobody enquires from the driver about the delay. Nothing decisive or creative happens until an hour later when there is a low and whining sound and the train jerks violently, shakes the people up and pulls away from the middle of nowhere headed to the next station.

TWO POEMS
by John Carse

My Demon Lover

I was seventeen
when first I saw The Stranger
a shadowy figure in a dream
a dark and dangerous enslaver
I strained to see him clearly
but his features were obscured
by a mist that became entangled
in the moon's dim light
in the self conscious dancing of the night

I've seen him in the flesh since then on beaches and in parks
in parked cars and darkened bars
and in my dreams he still appears
and from his eyes spring shooting stars
that drown among the tattoos on his arms
and from his mouth snakes slither
and hiss and kiss my mouth
and lick my scars

Enticing me closer
to the death he holds
within his wounded hands
and from his arms unfold
bouquets of tears
and from his broken feet arise
the fallen stars of all the years
and the silent explanation
of my hidden fears

Mother's Little Man

She used to sit on the bed
with one foot up
painting her toenails
while little puffs of cotton wool flowered
like miniature cauliflowers between her toes

when she curled her hair
using those ugly pink plastic rollers that were so common in those days
the astringent smell of perm fluid permeated not only her hair
but the air around her
as well

I remember the smell
of the used laddered stockings
that she left tangled among her shoes because I'd try them on
when she wasn't there
and wear her red stilettos
and strut my stuff

when she was out on the town
with another 'hot prospect'
and I was left alone
to rifle through the tampons
and scratched smooth nail files
and dried up cutex bottles
that cluttered her drawer

looking for loose change

TWO POEMS
by Mboneni Ike Muila

A sing along poem

A sing along poem
to a crazy kwala soul mangolongolo
silver high heel bell bottom-turn-up
character diza masheleni
midnight winter rainfall
without your own zozo or
mukhukhu shelter shack
to put up en sleep
kuya khomaza kulelo khomazo
even chickens know where to sleep
when the night comes
DK clovers bantwana shine umashesha mampela
twin town twinkling two door shimovana
crossover vuvuzela page jika jive
sishaya-ama-turnaround baby
let me see your figure
before the broken fragile face
of a picaso burst
iyo iyo lolo
lo thishara
hakana register
uzo sibhala phi..,
thitshere washu hoyu
uri funza u vhala
thitshere washu hoyu
uri funza u vhala
A na B na one na
Two three four five

Velevele

Vele
velevele „,
one thing for sure velevele is a statement of confirmation
landing without a warning
to the plains of no reasonable doubt
the move stamps out without saying
that i am only incommand of a spoken word
mixmasala mgosi chop chop my word
dwarsdeur mekaar chopper chopper chapies
mingle mence mence by en by
by my means meanwhile scrawling slicingcutting
en pasting mixmasala living word
across your fountain pen African language connection
if not so someone else is
under banners of isicamtho ground major I salute
binne pozi jumptyd drank jy smere-mere or jika skhambathi wise
hier is nou my dozen crate dark en lovely
mummy blues phola hierso
mjojo grend-grend moja
vele
velevele is die dae se goeters of die dinge
wat inspired me to write buddy scamtho
behind amabonda ne environment ya se kasi
langikhulela khona as a bambino had an
all round inspiring impact on me a lot
playing hide en seek blk mapatile no no game
people i associated myself with amongst gawe mense
comrade bras tigers van ou topies en taimas
wat slim is
a bo matwetwe moeg se kleva oneside
kom kry hulle dra die dae se vision forward en
hulle is capable to lead the way soos mense
wat ken hulle mission in life as buddies
van toeka se dae af vele
velevele nomakanjani kanjani mr know-it-all
ndangala spy poet in supreme isicamtho is a language
of survival no wordplay about vele „,velevele

Kodwa we – Goli

by Brian Bhengu

Sakhulwa kuhashwa kubatshazwa
Kutuswa futhi kunconya wena
Ababuya kuwe bengawu'vali umlomo
Ngobuhle nangobukhazikhazi bakho
Abangakwazi babekubona emaphusheni
Nangamehlo enqgondo kuphela
Wawufana nezwe lesethembiso.
Lapho kwakufezeka izifiso zabaningi
Wazigwinya wagoloza izingane zabantu
Obaba bakhohlwa yithi nenzalabantu.
Bashona emajukujukwini ekujuleni komhlaba
Bethi basebenzela izingane zabo
Kanti bafukuzela ondlebe zikhanyi'langa
Ukuthi baphucule ezabo izimpilo zodwana.
Awugcinanga lapho Goli ndini, uthe usuka
Wabiza udadewethu uNomathemba
Wamthembisa izulu nomhlaba,kanti ufuna
Alahlu'mlenze adayise ngomzimba wakhe.
Kuthe usumfimfithile umfwethu
Wamlahla phansi okwamafinyila
Wam'gugisa ngamankwebemvu wamqeda
Kodwa awuzibheke namhlanje
Ubukhotheni bakho, ukuphupha kwakho
Kazi kusekhona ukuseyigolide ngawe!
Njengoba usugugile usumabokoboko unje
Njengoba sewaguquk'umgqomo wezibi
Kanti ubuhle bakho babukuphi we Goli?
Waze waphupha kabi Goli!

Give

by Heinrich Böhmke

Velislav Milov started his own religion on the first day of March. Of course, he never planned such a preposterous thing. It happened in a fit of pique. Nevertheless, the signs were there to see. A stomach bug two days earlier had all but forced a fast upon him and there'd been a truly terrible storm the night before, the air humming with lightning and his dogs pissing themselves as thunder banged and rolled.

Sitting in the gloom of his house during the deluge, Milov had pondered the state of his life. He was sixty-six and the first year of his retirement was a disappointment. His health was failing. All the fantasies he had stored up, hoping to act upon at this stage of life, fantasies cherished, taken out from time to time during a working day like a matchbox car still in its cellophane covering and excitedly considered from all angles – were slipping beyond his reach. If it were not for its all year surfing, Milov would hardly have chosen Durban as the place to live on emigrating from Bulgaria as a young man. That activity was now impossible with the back pain. If it were not for the sultry Indian secretaries and salesgirls around every corner of the city, he'd long have married a nice white lady and had children to amuse him in his dotage. That activity, too, was now impossible, notwithstanding the efforts of modern chemistry. Poor health had robbed a bitter Milov of his earthly rewards for working so hard and getting so rich at a time when it was too late to do anything about it.

Velislav Milov had run a paint company with outlets all over Durban. Eleven years before, his driver had stopped to pick up a man looking for a lift. There was an accident and the man had been flung from the back of the bakkie into oncoming traffic. Milov needn't have taken responsibility. The dead man was a poor African togt-worker and the Road Accident Fund would sort the family out. Milov had paid bribes before, so if the family tried to sue, he was sure he could quash the case.

The wife came to see him a few months after the accident; with her were three serious little girls, the youngest barely walking. She had come to ask her husband's boss for his effects. The police had given the paint shop address on Stamford Hill. There was obviously a mix-up. Milov was not a generous man but he did make up his mind quickly. He decided there and then to pretend that the dead man had worked for him. By the time the woman and the six large accusing eyes had left, Milov had given orders for a monthly salary of the lowest paid worker in his factory to be sent to the widow.

"For how long, Mr Milov?" his general manager asked.

"For fucking ever," Milov replied – though he never knew why he had done this, it didn't matter because it was not a lot of money.

Over the next decade, Milov had sporadic contact with the family. Mostly the widow came alone to the office to ask for extra money to cover this or that emergency: an appendix operation, school fees every January and a deposit for a new outbuilding when the family was once evicted. He enjoyed these visits immensely, but couldn't help adopting an irritable tone from across the table when the widow was shown in. He thought it stripped the act of charity of schmaltz. It made giving and taking easier to bear. The brusqueness also discouraged excessive thank you's which Milov hated.

·

At the end of each year, Milov was treated to a visit from the girls. Their mom spoke to them rather sternly in Zulu in his presence, and after Milov smoothed his beard to a point and gruffly shoved some petty cash the way of the kids, saying, "share", the girls filed merrily out of the office till the following year. On these particular days, Milov was in the best possible mood he was ever in, outside of the Indian Ocean that is.

There had only been one unsatisfactory moment. The elder girl had hooked up with some township riff-raff. Accompanied by the girl, the much older man had come asking for a job. Milov hadn't liked the look of him - lopsided hat and gold tooth, through the one-way glass of his office - and refused to see them. He would have raised this unwelcome visit with the mother, except that that December, she brought only two daughters.

After selling the business, Velislav Milov had no more control over the pay-roll. He had not considered that the payments would stop with all the hundred and one other things he had to do when handing over the keys to the new owners. In time, the dead man's wife arrived at his house in Umhlanga. The gate guard was in the process of chasing her away, a diligence, Milov found out, he had shown twice before. On this occasion Milov was just nudging his Jag into the driveway. This time he told the guard it was okay and leaned over to open the passenger door for her, but she took too long to get in. Milov drove slowly down the milkwood lane to his front door with the widow following on foot behind.

And so began the monthly collections of envelopes of cash. Milov decided against a stop-order. It wasn't too much trouble drawing the money himself, and he didn't mind handing the money over personally, although they said you shouldn't. The visits were a nice distraction - it was so quiet about the house.

*

On the first of March (the day he unwittingly started a religion) Velislav Milov was in a foul mood. A storm had caused his dogs to wet the carpets, his back was sore and he had come to see that his retirement fantasies of surfing all morning, sleeping all afternoon and seducing Indian temptresses all night were impossible. He stood alone on his balcony, a stash of sunflower seeds in a carved bowl balanced on the railing and around his feet husks stripped expertly from the seed, as only a born Bulgarian knew how. From his balcony he could see the ocean. About a mile out it was churning brown and gooey green. The Umgeni River had dumped all the up-country filth into the sea with the big rain, not only sand but sewage and litter and industrial detritus. "What man doesn't do properly on land becomes the ocean's problem," Milov was thinking when the gate buzzer rang. It was the day the widow came to collect her money.

He had maintained the ritual of the desk. He invited her into the dining room and showed her a chair. Then he disappeared into another room as if to fetch the money when it was already in a folded envelope in his pants pocket. Returning, Milov faced the black woman sitting across from him.

"So how are the girls doing? Well, hey?"

Dolly (that was her name) nodded and smiled, "Ja, baba."

"Dolly, we haven't spoken about an increase in a long time. What do you say?"

On any other day, Milov would have slipped another hundred or two into the envelope but not today. Today, he'd make her ask him.

"Really, things are so hard at home," Dolly exclaimed more pointedly than ever.

"But how much extra do you want, Dolly, R20, R50, R100," Milov pushed her.

"I can't say, baba."

"Then tell me what you need the extra money for, then I will know how much you want."

Dolly eyed Milov for a second and then blurted, "The women in the church are going on a trip and it is costing R350. The food too is covered. But people who are going must pay by next Friday."

Milov had never before considered the possibility that any of the money he gave Dolly was spent on anything other than bare essentials. It was not a lot of money in the first place and, in his mind, all these years he had seen their rent being paid first, then his largesse putting vegetables and macaroni and maybe some chicken on the table of "his" dead worker. He also envisaged them using the money for some second-hand clothes and the stuff women needed. Now, in an instant, it occurred to him that Dolly and the girls may be entertaining themselves and others on his money. By her own admission, Dolly was part of a church group. By township standards, Dolly may actually be quite well off with a regular salary coming in. What if she was giving money out to undeserving causes? These ideas all fired through Milov's mind in an inchoate way, more as a vague feeling of being taken for granted than an express objection to any specific instance.

"A church group? Are you part of a church?"

Dolly misread Milov's tone as enthusiasm and beamed as she said, "Yes, baba, since my husband died, we go to church together. We were crying all the time and the pastor he did help us. We go to church every Sunday, me and my children."

Milov felt blood rise to his face. When he spoke he heard his voice sharpen with the same indignation he felt welling up inside.

"What do you mean, the pastor helped you …? Tell me, Dolly, please tell me honestly, how much do they charge you to be part of that church of yours?"

Dolly was flummoxed. "They don't charge nothing, sir."

Dolly looked worried now. She was a clever woman. She had caused offence, but was struggling to see what she must do to rectify the situation.

"So you don't give any money to the pastor?"

"No, nothing." Dolly was categorical.

Velislav Milov felt a pang of relief and the beginnings of embarrassment set in. He had over-reacted. He had been silly.

But then Dolly added, "We only give tithes, (she said the word in two syllables). But the ti-thes is not for the pastor, it is for the church."

Ah you stupid woman, Milov felt like screaming. This unusual anger was back but somehow Milov kept from exploding.

"Tell me Dolly, how many people come to your church?"

"About thirty, no, more now, fifty."

"Yes, fifty, and where do you go for church?"

"In a garage. They stole our tent so we have service in the pastor's garage."

This time Milov could not help himself, "Ah, you stupid woman!"

Dolly was terrified now. She was literally quaking in her chair.

"I'm sorry Dolly, I shouldn't have said that. Look at me. I'm not cross with you." Milov took a deep breath. "I just want you to answer me one more thing. How much do you give the church every month?"

Dolly had an answer she could give, a factual answer, amidst this fury which she didn't understand.

"A ti-the, I give a ti-the."

Milov rocked back in his chair so hard it scraped.

"You have been giving some two-bit pastor ten percent of your money, my money, for the last ten years?"

Dolly's head was on her chest. She may have been weeping. It only encouraged Milov's rage.

"What the fuck for?" he continued. "What has he ever done for you? Are you crazy, Dolly. It's a scam. Your bloody pastor should be locked-up."

And then a thought struck Milov.

"And he's probably been saying that your good luck in getting money, money from the white man, is because of him. That's what you think, isn't it, isn't it Dolly? Huh? Today's Sunday, did you pray at church with the pastor that the mlungu will give you an increase, Dolly? More ti … thes! Jesus Christ, what a joke".

Milov was aware that his behaviour was off the wall. But something inside him had obviously snapped and the thing was, it felt so good. Living alone, working in a professional environment all these years, he hardly ever had the opportunity to vent. Milov was not a militant atheist. He would never have bothered with anyone else's religious beliefs if he wasn't funding them. But there was no use screaming at Dolly. These people were so easy to fool. Look at what the missionaries had done to them and nothing had ever changed in four gullible centuries.

While Dolly quietly sobbed, Milov went to the kitchen, pressed one glass against the water dispenser on the door of the fridge and then another. He returned to the dining-room where Dolly looked up, a fat, pathetic tear running out from under her glasses. He pushed a glass of water over to her and sat down. The storm was over but Milov was as engaged as ever.

"I am sorry Dolly. I should not have shouted at you. You have done nothing wrong. It's your money. You can do what you want with it."

Dolly made as if to get up. This scene had really frightened her. God knows what the security guard would think seeing her leave in this state.

"Before you go, Dolly, I want to explain something to you. It is not your pastor who has looked after you and your girls for ten years. It is me. I am your pastor, Dolly. On Sundays when you get up and dress nicely, and take a taxi, (do you take a taxi to church, Dolly?), ah yes, when you take a taxi to church and sing nice songs and pray and smile, it should be to me that you are coming by taxi to sing songs in your nice clothes."

Milov had meant to be sarcastic but he found the words he spoke to be perfectly sincere.

"Think about it. Who is giving you something and getting nothing, nothing in return?"

Dolly was staring at Milov and he saw the words hitting home. She seemed to nod as she listened to him speak. The tears had dried.

*

The following weekend Milov went to a House and Home show in Jo'burg. He'd been invited by Dulux. They probably didn't know he'd retired. On the second Sunday after his outburst, Milov's first congregation arrived. The security guard buzzed him from the gate to ask if he should let them in. They were asking for Pastor Milov. It was Dolly, two girls and an elderly couple, maybe man and wife, dressed very nicely. He lead them to seats at the dining room table and he stood at its head. At eleven o'clock in the morning, Milov finished talking to them. It was an easy if uninspiring sermon consisting of a list of predictions. The economy was bad, jobs would be lost, violence ahead of elections would increase. The one specific unexpected prediction Milov knew would impress them for next week was that the lotto price would go up to R3.50 (he'd heard this from a guy at House and Home who was a big shot in the Lotto). He ended by saying that everyone should love their neighbour and not envy them if they had livestock.

Milov's was going to be a practical ministry. After they prayed, he took everyone into his triple garage. There was so much stuff there that he had no more use for. A lawnmower, TV sets, two dusty computers, golf clubs, surfboards, toolboxes, a settee, antique light fittings (an old girlfriend was obsessed), books, CD's, litres of paint, shoes, boxes of clothes and linen, including three new Armani suits and a motorbike that needed a mechanic to give it the once over. He stood with his congregation in front of these goods. They could each take what they could carry away. In time, when the garage was empty, there'd be food and there'd be cash.

Truth be told, Milov had found the first service quite stilted. He was unprepared for it. He and his congregation still had to figure out properly how they would sing and pray. Today had not been very satisfactory in that regard. But worshipping at Velislav Milov's church was still new to them all. He knew the innate African musical ability and sense of occasion would soon come to the fore and that future services would be emotionally moving events. He'd also like to see the congregation grow. Thirty to fifty was a good number to aim for. Once all of these things were in place - his congregation's praise and worshipping on the one hand and bestowing real and immediate blessings on the other - Pastor Milov would start working on some new material for moral guidance. There were lessons to be learned from surfing and the mixing of paints. The Bible was getting outdated.

Before they left with black bags of their chosen blessings, Milov thought it would be a good idea to say a final prayer. He thought of Dolly and how she had ended up enriching his life in so many ways. Through her Milov had got to play the role of a grandfather or uncle to her kids. Later, their intense discussion had put him on this present religious course for which he was very grateful. His life had a new meaning at the moment when he thought all meaning was lost. Closing off the prayer, Milov asked that God protect the soul of Dolly's dear spouse who had been such an excellent employee.

The security guard looked bemused and just a little jealous as the group of five walked up the drive with their bags. The old man who had come along had difficulty carrying his sack of clothes. Milov asked if he needed help as he lagged behind. The old man smiled brightly and said thank you, but no, they had transport waiting just around the corner. It was Dolly's husband in his taxi.

THREE POEMS
by Lara Potgieter

epiphanies

there are moments
when we stumble
upon our own
insignificance

and it slaps us
so hard
through the face

that we forget
what we have seen

and we turn around
and we begin
again.

the darkness

the tears
that run
from the danger
of the day,

the effusion
 that sleeps
til the dark's
done its due -

it's the tearing apart
of the tapestry
of thought

of the girl
who's been told
that there is
no such thing

as darkness
made dark
by darkness
alone.

the party

all the pretty talk
adorned in alcohol
and scattered amongst
arrangements of shapes and space

debris of capsized thought
in a junkyard of failed significance

incubated ideas
that grow into fleshless words

solitary soldiers
waving their chosen flags –
ballads of belief
to lull their sleeping beasts

calculated candlelight
to complement
the deadweight decency
of fitted shirt and tie

handshakes and handjobs
for the helpless hero
who comes here
to join the other lonely ones

in their endless avoidance
of the infinite insight
of isolation.

African Soldiers

by Jean-Francois Kouadio

As soon as the soldiers released the composition their government, newspapers close to the opposition Socialist Party start without delay their offensive. The front page of The Direct reads: New government: Foreigners seize the power. And in the columns, the "venomous" journalist author of the article erects the genealogical tree of each minister and openly states their foreign origins.

It is known to all that a sheep-like attitude always calls a shepherd reaction. Logically, the new minister in charge of the fight against tribalism and the total eradication of xenophobia, the unbendable sergeant, pardon the Minister Bokaya, summons the author of the article and the editor of the paper.

The two pressmen respond to the minister's convocation without delay. They arrive at the minister's office where there's no need to mention the impressive presence of some infantrymen armed up to the teeth. In his massive office that hardly suits him; the sergeant-minister Bokaya is comfortably sitting behind a large, shinning and first grade wooden desk. Once the journalists introduced in the office, he roars on a terrifying warlike tone:

"You two there! If you have no proof, you are dead! Stop, right there!"

Ten meters separate the journalists from the irascible minister.

"What are your fucken proofs? I know what you two imbeciles are suffering from: xenophobia and tribalism! This is the last time I'm asking the question! What are your damn fucken proofs?"

"None?"

The minister stared at them with his red-blood injected eyes and concludes: "Good!"

The two men instinctively scratch the back of their head. They do not how to start the explanations. The impatient minister Bokaya goes for the speed dial button on his desk phone. Two seconds elapse. The door of his office opens with an extreme brutality behind the journalists. Before the editor turns his neck to locate the noise, a violent hammer-blow well adjusted hits the back of his head. He faints on the ground. The escaping soul shakes is body like decapitated chicken in agony. The journalist, author of the article instinctively jumps towards the minister Bokaya to escape from another soldier who chases his on a few meters. The journalist raises his arms as a sign of surrender. "Ha!" The hypocenter of his forehead crashes again the iron bar thrown by his aggressor. From his left eyebrow, a stream of blood pours like a water tap. He too faints and falls about two meters next to desk of the minister Bokaya who watches impassive the horrible scene that yet, seems to gratify him. He says on a firm tone to his "disciples": "Do not finish them here, take them to the camp! Get me someone to clean this blood on the wall! Now get out of here!!"

Outside the office, the two pressmen are dragged on the rough ground till the basement of the building where they are precipitated in the boot of a military van. Three guards watching the entrance of the basement jump into the van as well. In the banal tumult of the CBD where the vehicle slowly disappears, no passerby can imagine what has just happened to those who dare criticize the new government, who dare disagree with the ministry in charge of the fight against tribalism and xenophobia. The military truck has just been running for two minutes when a soldier says, deceived:

"Damn! These fuckers are already dead".

"Then only fuck cares! Dead here or at the camp, it makes no fucken difference"! Articulate another squaddy.

"You are damn right! We just need to know where to dump these fucken bodies, that's all"!

The military camp of the first battalion of artillery soon supplants the justice court of Abidjan. The soldiers have truly decided to eradicate tribalism and xenophobia. They have maliciously created in that military camp a "court of exception" of which most military magistrates' academic level does not go beyond that of grade 4 of the primary school kids. This court of exception, officially in charge of judging the tribalists, the sectarians, well, those who do not understand the redeeming political strategy of the military regime will quickly be transformed into an instant justice system where no law is used to fix the law. The squaddies' court even has a toll free number available twenty-four/seven. Is your neighbor sleeping with your wife? Do not panic. Just call the juridical-police. In just fifteen minutes, a whole bunch of idle infantrymen piled in a military truck will pay a visit to your wife's secret lover. The soldiers will properly wash his butt before questioning him. If that day, they are in a bad mood, the cheater can loose his life given the myriad of blows pitilessly stricken. The soldiers are so well organized that they have created a number of specializations inside the military camp.

Dial the number of the brigade "black dragon"; if you wish your debtor to pay back your money in ten minutes. Do not hesitate to call the brigade "Puma", if your neighbor slanders the new government, this is the proof he hates the ethnic group to which belongs the honorable colonel president. Then in five little minutes, such gossip will be drug before the redeeming court of exception to explain his "tribalistic" and xenophobic attitudes. Are you jealous of someone who is married to a beautiful woman? Then, you can directly address your complaint to the brigade "Camora" who will come and punish the man who is unfairly, unjustly and illegally the husband of a beautiful woman.

The minister in charge of the fight against tribalism directly deals with the nation's delicate questions related to high rank noisy politicians or boiling and excited journalists. The soldiers, pardon the military-judges never argue; as the thief is afraid of the light, they have a wild adversity for those who reason.

The whole week that follows the murder of the two journalists, the militia of the sergeant minister Bokaya, composed of some young marijuana enslaved squaddies showed no mercy in a popular shantytown of Abidjan. There, a man owed two thousand frank CFA to a cousin his. According to a newspaper author of the information, the aforementioned cousin who needed the sum of money to clear an urgent domestic matters run out of patience, called the juridical police to ensure a quick recovery of his cash. People say the debtor lost an eye during the legal brutality that authorizes the recovery of the debt. This is the proof given by the government that the recreation is over.

Guéyo's government has resolutely decided to put an end to the state of impunity erected by the overthrown president Baziana. They have instead decided to work hard. The National Broadcasting Corporation, now exclusive loudspeaker of the squaddies gets sadistically innovative. This day, at the inauguration of the national campaign against AIDS, Guéyo proves it in his address to the nation. In fact the fight against H.I.V, xenophobia and tribalism are the major axes of his governmental program. Guéyo himself said that tribalism and xenophobia are the two most serious blights on Ivory Coast. That's why he created a minister in charge of the struggle against xenophobia and the total eradication of tribalism in Ivory Coast. Here is unfolded the content of the ambitious program of President Guéyo's team.

"To hell with the Economy! The economy can wait! It's only when there's peace between citizens and if they are not dead of H.I.V that they can sit and discuss economic matters."

Good heavens! Guéyo is really a political genius; how can a "sick" national economy provide food in households as weak as those of the shantytowns? Only he knows the secret formula that explains his political choices. This sentence spitted by the colonel Guéyo, at the inauguration of the national campaign against AIDS, falls right into the sensitive ears of the entire nation. In fact the sentence is nothing else than the summary of the forward-looking governmental program.

This afternoon, Guéyo says to the population of a shantytown called "Soweto" massed on a crowded soccer playground.

"Dear compatriots, Have you ever seen Dieudonné Baziana in this neighborhood?"

"No!" Shouts back a colonized crowd.

"Well, we want to fight against AIDS together; and we want you to know that this new government likes you all! We are different from those who think that people of shantytowns are not real citizens of this country."

"Guéyo! Guéyo! Guéyo!" Shouts a euphoric crowd, satisfied that the central political power itself has decided to come closer to the masses, to listen to their worries.

"You, the youth, you are the future of Ivory Coast, I beg you; please protect yourselves. Use condoms, if not AIDS will kill you".

•

Although Mary Cathy, former Miss Ivory Coast, was known as the goddess of lust and tricks, no one understood how she managed to mingle with the cream of the new military-political system. This afternoon, she is sitting comfortably under the gigantic tent a row behind the Colonel President Guéyo. Once the ceremony marking the launch of the campaign against AIDS is over, she escorts the presidential delegation to a private place. The colonel in person invites her, far from Mrs. Guéyo's indiscreet watch, for a tête-à-tête in one of the confiscated villas of the overthrown president, Dieudonné Baziana. After dinner, she congratulates Guéyo for his great heart and his compassion for the poor population of precarious neighborhoods. She openly offers to gather all the women of Ivory Coast in what she calls the National Women Squad Against AIDS, as proof of her interest in communitarian actions. Between two resonant belches, caused by the delicate savoring of a divine White Muscadet, the French cognac the couple was sharing, Guéyo noisily slams the voluminous tongue that clutters his palace and says, "I was planning to appoint you as a national high commissioner in charge of the fight against AIDS. You could supervise and educate the women of Ivory Coast. How's that?"

The ex-Miss Ivory Coast skillfully opens her velvet-like thighs. The brightness of her corrupting underwear nearly busts the wide eyes of the muzzled colonel. She slowly crosses her wooden-brown, barely covered legs and smiles. She then offers some white and perfectly aligned teeth as if not designed for food. She goes on in a frail voice.

"My General…oh pardon me, my President, I welcome your proposal. I simply regret not being able to thank you proportionally."

Meanwhile, the colonel pours himself another adult dose of the French cognac, empties the glass in a single shot and pulls the corners of his mouth to express his satisfaction. He belches once again and tries to focus. One can clearly see that Guéyo struggles to do so, since the cognac has already kicked off a real internal combat inside him. The president smiles, leans towards his guest and says without diplomacy or courtesy, "Listen, you can sleep here tonight."

In truth, Mary Cathy is more or less prepared for such a proposal – for this is her most formidable weapon. Yet she wasn't expecting such total gaucheness from the president. Nonetheless, she quickly gathers herself. She surely did not come this close to the looming goal to let it go!

"That's OK my Gene…oh! I am feeling very uncomfortable, I am disgusted with myself… I am forever confusing 'Colonel', 'President' and 'General'… Sorry, Your Excellency".

These mistakes of the former Miss Ivory Coast, far from provoking wrath, end up suggesting some new ideas to Guéyo. He laughs loudly.

"Ah, ah, ah! You speak like some provincial delegates I met yesterday. They said I deserve to be a General. A Head of State never refuses the will of the people; the people will promote me to the rank of General very soon. I am sure of that."

With that the young and beautiful woman joins him on the silky divan. The expert knows that when mental structures of most males are disconnected by ethanol, their blood circulates faster in the lower parts of the stomach. Not so subtly, she thrusts her supple hands under the president's ample robe and meets the obstacle of his rebellious tool – it is inflated with desire. Once the soft fingers of Mary Cathy touch his equipment, the colonel releases a deep sigh as if the unforgiving blade of a sharp knife was chopping his flesh. With the agility of a professional tool sucker, she gently and greedily takes his member between her warm lips. The emotion is at it highest peak. Under the skilful pressure of her supple touches, Guéyo, fearing that he might release sooner than he should, tries to contain the hungry female. He deepens his butt in the divan to prevent the spasm from taking him by surprise; Mary Cathy strikes back by pulling the honorable presidential underwear with both hands. Guéyo tries desperately to grasp her slim hand as if at this stage of the operation, she could even escape.

"I am here Your Excellency. I won't leave." She tries to provide assurance with an additional and convincing smile.

Guéyo can barely hear her and Mary Cathy soon realizes the pain she is causing to the unfortunate master of Ivory Coast. She lies on her back on the divan and quietly contemplates the beating presidential tool. She still has her clothes on. She knows the starters are over. She knows it is the last step before the main course has to be dished out. She then logically introduces an ultimate request.

"My President, do you have … do you by any chance have a condom?"

"What??" Guéyo is more than surprised.

"I mean, a protective device…you know, a condom." Mary Cathy tries to be clearer.

"A Condom? Absolutely not! Condoms are for youngsters."

In that instant he turns his utmost attention to the removal of the transparent G-string that adorns her loins. After all, why waste time on more talk about this unnecessary burden, this device needed only by youngsters? And Mary Cathy keeps quiet while General-to-Be, President Guéyo, the toughest enemy of H.I.V and AIDS in all of the Ivory Coast, in a single lunge deploys his powerful tool into her wet but ticklish intimacy. But sadly, the presidential paunch soon bothers the delicate assault and Mary Cathy decides to take the initiative. By means of a series of well adjusted, rapid but short sequences of athletic hip shakes, she soon obtains some noisy mumbles from the poor fellow. Suddenly, a voluptuous spasm, on its way to hell, crosses and shakes his body and his breath goes raspy; great, strong and unbearable is his pleasure.

"Heuuuurg!"

Then Guéyo, while releasing an incandescent flood of seed, follows this groan with an abundant flow of saliva. The firm chest of the young woman is soon flooded. Guéyo sweats abundantly in spite of the air-conditioning. Only wealth, promises of social promotion, can humiliate such a beautiful creature. The lady looks at him with an ironic smile. She is, despite herself, glad to have managed to floor in a single grip the master of Ivory Coast; she is happy that an ugly man like Guéyo, who was only able to possess her thanks to his stature in the national arena, did not prolong the difficult and painful comedy.

After he has managed to catch his breath Guéyo wipes his muzzle with the back of a wrinkled hand and says, "That was good, very good indeed".

Indeed.

TWO POEMS
by Akiva Zasman

The Visit

Remembering my late brother. How I picked him up at an airfield one afternoon in autumn- this going back eight maybe nine years.
He'd managed to 'hitch' a lift with a pilot friend of his in a white and blue Cessna.
They're not very large those planes. The two of them came bouncing and spluttering down the runway. He limped to my car, exaggerating the cramped conditions of the cockpit. I offered him a cigarette as he extracted a bottle of whisky from his Lowepro camera bag. He'd arrived that day from the town he was living and working in as a press photographer. I was fairly young then, I didn't know what it was like to have a job- how the pressure can get to you sometimes. When later that night after he'd returned from a pub near my flat, I had to help him out of the bath.
He retched into the water. I brought him the towel he'd left on the bed.

Charles De Gaulle Airport, 2005
After a poem by Ezra Pound)

The appearance of these faces in the crowd
carrying Pick 'n Pay "green bags"
                   like foliage on some familiar tree.

FOUR POEMS
by Ahmed Patel

Miserly Exaltation

Getting no answers whatsoever
  Alas!
The silent soldier's smouldering corpse
Naked to God; dishonoured by man
Hopeless situations
Require hopeful solutions

Crawling Insects

She creeps slowly back into bed
The smell of sex connects them
  Faint connection
Time for the post-fuck reflection
Flick... suck... blow
The smoke settles with ease

Homemade Remedy

Have no faith in the world
Command
Only straying eyes touch down
On broken promises
There is no life or purpose
Beyond your narcissistic shackles

Go Away

Time carelessly moulds a sitting man
Into his father's father's father
Lousy life
Fart-ridden, stale sleep
Lost perception of perfection
Gormless collection of truths

TWO POEMS
by Selwyn Ramsdale

Mowbray Terminus

late afternoon under a sky
inflated by the sulphurous mess
of scorched fuels.
the pensioner in patched leather jacket
and black-rimmed spectacles, fidgets
with a packet of red-skinned peanuts,
waits impatiently for the Bridgetown bus.
another man in ragged sports jacket
and frayed shirt, lights up a cigarette,
clenches a plastic bag between arm and ribs.
mother and son unfurl a parcel
of hot chips and penny polonies.
the fetid steam wafts along the wall
contaminated by the vulgar desperation
of bored students and
hip-hop graffiti.
and so we endure
the pollution of diesel fumes.
the grit of oil on tar.
the wait.

Eight Goals

i once let in eight goals
in a game. there were
mitigating circumstances:
the opponents were older
and more skilful. my father
ignored these factors
when he humiliated me
in front of my friends.
i returned with a sharp
word or two. in avoiding
a punch from him
i caused a fracture
of his wrist.

these are the lessons
we inevitably learn.
masculine challenges
and inadvertent
consequences.

The Acquisitionist
by David Kerr

As Kadar rolled out of the Kulturburo he glanced at the Pillage Permit flashing yellow on his pulsar. It took only two days to pick up the Outland visa, his jabs, a couple of well-armed Intrazone pacifiers from New Nairobi, a portacraft, a few hand-tools, and some immicredits. Not that Kadar was new to Outland. His first visa had been for the Chittagong murals. He'd needed a whole platoon of pacifiers to procure the art work. But it was worth it. The pulsar A rate for South Asian murals had gone up 0.0137 after that acquisition. Then there'd been the Michiko masks and most successful of all, the Kisangali Mama Wati prints.

This was the smallest expedition Kadar had ever led. The lanky, male pacifier, with the stupid nom-de-guerre, Dragon, doubled up as driver. The other, Kamoto, a stocky Amazon, was their local linguist, though in Kadar's experience, Outlander dialects changed so fast, she might have a tough time.

Basically, Kadar's niche had been carved out of the Kulturburo's negligence during Partition. The Buro had assumed that post-Partition aesthetics would be conservative, hankering for the great European, Central Asian, North African and Chinese classics – a Noah's ark collection of elegance from stable eras before fiscal Armageddon. In a way they were right, but the kulturiks had failed to anticipate an interesting backlash, Inlander curiosity for submerged byways of pre-Partition world culture. At first the kulturiks were suspicious of Kadar, with his folklore interests and expertise in Outlander naiferie. But the pulsar rates dictated terms, and he started getting contracts – to fill the Buro's acquisition gaps.

Dragon slowed the portacraft down when they reached the gate. Their destination, a large village, called Namadzi ("in-the-water" according to Kamoto) was close to the partition wall, as the 6th vector Inland corridor connecting the Eastern and Southern blocks, snaked down the Rift Valley. The nearest gate, however, was about three hundred kilometers to the South at Tete on the Zambezi.

Kadar's quest seemed hay-stack-needlish, but he trusted his good nose for acquisitions. The grail was a 1998 Ngwiri ball-point sketch. Solomon Ngwiri was probably Kadar's greatest achievement; the African artist's mukwa sculptures, wax-print textiles, and his last period, line-drawing portraits adorned Inland's finest Kultur houses. Fortunately for the artist's reputation, Kadar had assiduously collected Ngwiriana during the transition to Partition. But even Kadar couldn't believe the astronomical rise in Ngwiri's recent A ratings, especially for the drawings. The free-flow of those peasant portraits seemed to hit some chord of Insider nostalgia for a lost world of simple human harmony.

Kadar flashed his Outland visa and his security number. Dragon switched on the shield, the gate opened and the craft eased out. Kadar had left Inland many times, but the shock of exit never ceased to affect him. The ride from New Nairobi had been exquisite, the herds of zebra, elephants and wildebeest teeming in the Rift Valley grasslands, were stunningly vivid. As soon as they went through the gate, however, the early morning air, dense with shooter tree smoke, flecked sooty particles onto the portacraft screen, which Dragon had to periodically wipe. A gang of Outsider juveniles, as if waiting for any crafts, hurled a few stones, which bounced harmlessly off the shield. Though twinges of conscience sometimes pricked his comfortable life, Kadar had no real sympathy for them; like all Insiders he had the arguments for Partition by heart.

Dragon headed the craft north, keeping the corridor wall to his starboard. They passed over numerous fires, several trudging lines of forced labour gangs, and, near Lunzu, one vicious spear skirmish, next to a contested well. Kamoto occasionally switched the vidi controls to manual to zoom up a closer picture. Kadar had learned about the missing Ngwiri drawing from an unpublished, Pre-partition memoir written by Julian Gray, an English friend of the artist. Kadar's excitement on paging through the memoir was intense.

> One day I got a lift from Sollie to go shopping in Blantyre. On the way
> back he insisted on stopping at every little road-side bar for a beer. In
> one place, at a dive called the Sharp Sharp Nightclub, Sollie latched
> onto a beautiful bar-girl, whose name I still recall – Doreen. He fondled
> her breasts and bought her beer, but she always wriggled free, as if
> she belonged on a higher plane. Then Sollie suddenly changed
> his mood. He grabbed an empty cigarette packet and tore it open, told
> Doreen to sit still on the bar stool, took a biro from his safari jacket,
> and drew a miniature portrait of her on the inside of the packet. It was
> a stunning profile, executed in less than three minutes, but expressing
> Doreen's character precisely. When he'd finished, he threw the packet
> at her. She picked it up and the other girls crowded round to admire.
> Doreen ecstatically hugged the packet and pushed it in her blouse
> between her breasts. Sollie and I finished our drinks and left, with me
> feeling deflated, at the thought of that masterpiece still sticking to the
> bar-girl's sweaty body.

Kadar wanted that miniature as if it was the Rosetta Stone and Benin bronzes all wrapped together. He knew that Doreen might have just used the cigarette packet to light a fire. But somehow, he felt not. From Gray's description Kadar had a hunch that she'd treasured the pure image of herself and kept it safe.

The portacraft reached Namadzi by 9.30. It was a squalid settlement, surviving on a primitive cig industry. The only sign of water was a filthy stream trickling through the village. There was a mob of juveniles at the landing site who seemed more curious than hostile. To be on the safe side, Dragon let off a low level acoustic blast, and the mob ran screaming for cover behind a tobacco-drying shed. Kadar stayed onboard while Dragon and Kamoto, in their silver protection suits, reccied the area. Kadar wriggled into his own suit, the visor protecting from pollution as well as missiles. The pacifiers came back to the craft to pronounce Namadzi safe. Dragon activated a parking guard for the craft and the three of them walked past staring crowds to the Boma.

The commandant was an ingratiating man, obsessed with finding out if Kadar had any immicredits. Kadar had no intention of saying he had. One Australian expedition was wiped out in old Port Moresby by rioters trying to get Inland clearance. Kadar had a difficult time explaining to the Commandant what he wanted. Kamoto tried in Chinyanja, the local lingua franca.

"A bar-girl called Doreen?" the Commandant began to mull. "1998? That's long before Partition."

Without a surname he thought it would be difficult. He summoned three elderly men. Kadar and Kamoto removed their visors to encourage communication. Kamoto asked the men about the Sharp Sharp nightclub. There was some ribald laughter. They asked for pandrex. Kadar pulled out a strip. After they started chewing, the stories began to crystallize about the good old days. One of the men seemed to recall that Doreen had got married to a Chiradzulu man, but it hadn't lasted. More pandrex and the memories flowed even stronger.

Gibson, a toothless farm drone, smelling foully of kachasu, recalled that after the failure of her childless marriage, Doreen had become very religious. She had joined a nantongwe spirit possession group, emerging as the leader of Mizimu ya Moyo, an ancestral cult attracting many followers during the trauma of Armageddon. She had also changed her name to Chisoni, which Kamoto translated as "Compassion". Gibson believed he knew some surviving members of Mizimu ya Moyo, even though the cult had declined rapidly after Chisoni's death.

Kadar persuaded the commandant to allow him, Gibson, Kamoto and Dragon to travel by donkey cart to a nearby hamlet, the center of Mizimu ya Moyo. While they were waiting for the donkey cart, hundreds of villagers gathered in a circle, silent except for a rumbling, accusatory murmur. Occasionally a beggar would venture forward, displaying blind eyes, pock-marked back, or polio-twisted legs. Dragon had to let off an acoustic blast to keep the circle at a distance. Kadar was glad of the visor, not just for the smell, but to insulate himself from persistent twinges of guilt. When the four of them left on the creaking cart, the murmur turned into jeering.

It took less than an hour's bone-jolting journey past stunted maize fields and dreary plantations of shooter trees to reach Chisoni's village. The reception here, rather than hostile was simply stunned. Several children ran away screaming, obviously their first time to see Inlanders. Gibson went to a few ramshackle mud huts to ask questions, before announcing that he'd located some Mizimu ya Moyo members. Before he would take them there he demanded an immicredit. Kadar had to suppress his laughter. Gibson, with his decrepitude, lack of both English and usable Inland skills, had not the slightest chance of passing through immiscreening. Kadar lied that he would source the immicredit if they found what they were looking for.

Gibson, grumbling, took them to a hut on the edge of the village, next to a steep outcrop of rocks. He called "Odi!", and after a while a gaunt woman, probably in her sixties came out wearing a tattered robe and monkey-skin hat. She greeted them in her language, and went inside the house, emerging with reed mat, which she spread under the shade of a mango tree. From the mat they could see another woman behind the shack, roasting mice on a fire of maize stalks and shooter twigs.

From Kamoto's enquiries it seemed their host, Namalenga, was the current leader of Mizimu ya Moyo. She declined Kadar's offer of pandrex. Kadar, his heart beginning to pound with a hunter's adrenalin, instructed Kamoto in the line of questioning – to probe back to 1998, and the incident of Ngwiri's sketch. Namalenga became increasingly uneasy about the questions. Kadar asked Kamoto what the problem was.

"This woman doesn't want to contemplate the time before Doreen's religious conversion."

"Why not?"

"Chisoni is like a messiah to these people, they can't imagine her a prostitute."

Kadar was surprised at the subtlety of Kamoto's analysis.

"We know Doreen probably died of AIDS, like Ngwiri and much of the population, but to her followers she was a virgin who was taken by the spirits to be a bride. They worship her."

"Have you asked about the portrait?"

"Yes. Namalenga just blanks out the possibility of Chisoni being in a bar."

Kadar began to lose heart. The portrait must have been destroyed within days of its creation. Or Gibson might be wrong about Doreen and Chisoni being the same woman. The whole expedition was probably a waste of energy.

Namalenga spoke again.

"She's inviting you to see the shrine they have for Chisoni."

Despite his crumbling hopes, Kadar couldn't completely quell his curiosity. He suggested going without Gibson and Dragon. Namalenga said the party would also have to include her daughter, Nkhondo, who was the shrine's main custodian. Namalenga called out to the younger woman, who kicked the fire out and took the roast mice into the hut. When she joined them she was wearing a crown of leaves and carried a gourd. Dragon was not happy with the idea of splitting the party, but Kadar over-ruled him.

Nkhondo led the way over the bare and rocky hill, then steeply down a dried-out stream-bed, which led to what once must have been a lake, containing an island of trees. They walked across the cracked mud and entered a wood of shooter trees. In the middle of the wood was an even denser copse of indigenous trees, and a few graves. Kadar guessed the copse had only escaped the axe because of Outland superstition about Mizimu ya Moyo. The path was little used, and they had to duck under tangles of creepers and whippy branches. At the center of the copse was a two metre high cairn of undressed stones, held together with dried mud. A canopy made of reeds and chicken feathers dangled over the top part of the shrine. Despite noon sunshine filtering through the branches, it was cool in the copse. Instinctively, Kadar and Kamoto spoke in whispers.

Nkhondo put her gourd down on a stone in front of the shrine. She and Namalenga knelt down and started a sing-song chant. Kamoto failed to interpret the prayer because it was not in Chinyanja. When it was over, Nkhondo stood up and removed the canopy. Kadar's heart suddenly roared with delirious joy. Inbedded in the shrine, within a frame of shells, broken pieces of old beer bottles and shiny, pre-Partition Coca Cola bottle tops, and protected from the rain by a strip of cracked glass, was the Ngwiri portrait of Doreen. The style was unmistakable. The quick ball-point scribbles and cross-hatching, condensed to the size of the cigarette packet, evoked Doreen's extraordinary dignity, an almost luminous self-assurance snatched from that fiendish bar.

No longer whispering, Kadar asked Kamoto to interpret. He could offer both Namalenga and Nkhondo immicredits, if they would allow him to take the picture of Doreen. He would use his personal clout to ensure the success of immiscreening. They could become Kultur dancers or artists. Anything. He'd sort that out later.

Kamoto began to translate the offer. Still kneeling on their haunches, Nkhondo and Namalenga glanced at each other, emitting an occasional ideophonic squeal. Namalenga replied.

"They re refusing, sir" Kamoto interpreted. "They say they're only interested in preserving the shrine and praying to Chisoni's spirit to intervene with the spirits."

"But this is crazy. Nobody refuses entry to Inland. They'll lead comfortable lives. No pollution. No fights over water. They won't have to live in a leaky shack or eat roast mice. They'll have the best of everything."

"They seem very determined."

The two women turned back to the shrine, and started singing. Of course Kadar could just pull down the flimsy cairn and tear out the drawing by hand. He had his pillage permit. But something about the song restrained him. It swelled and ebbed, then throbbed more intensely again. The women's faces glowed with a fervour Kadar never saw in Inland, except in classic works of religious or erotic art.

Nkhondo poured frothy grey beer from the gourd onto the ground in front of the shrine. The women began clapping. The beer soaked into the soil and the song seemed to reach a climax of liquid intensity. Kadar stared at the portrait and it flared back like a pure flame. A cold tingle of recognition went down his spine. He had been to the pyramids, Stonehenge, Beijing, Matu Pichu, but they had all seemed sanitised. This was totally different, like a rivulet that was yet the source of a mighty river.

The song came to an end and the women stood up. Kadar, with a cleansed feeling almost of relief, turned to Kamoto.

"Don't tell Dragon what we saw. Let's go back. Mission unsuccessful."

Kamoto's eyes flickered then went coldly complicit. She too, touched by the ceremony, seemed to fully understand Kadar's inaction. Silently, they made their way out of the trees into the noon sunshine.

Away From The Dead

by Karen Jennings

Rumours spread among the workers that the farm had been sold. The old man, dead two weeks previously, had left the farm to his children; children who lived in cities overseas; who had no interest in farming. In that respect, the workers comforted each other, the sale of the farm was a good thing. For what good could have come from it being run by those who did not know how? Yet, behind the words of reassurance, they worried privately. Would they keep their current wages? How much would change? And most importantly, would the new owners keep them all on?

Before long the answer came. None would remain. Farming was an expensive and unreliable business. The new owners, property developers, explained in letters addressed to each individual worker that money could no longer be made from farming. Climate change, the expense of irrigation, regulations with regard to pesticides, all of these made farming too much of a liability. Money, the developers asserted, came from having something people wanted to buy. Therefore they had chosen to build luxury holiday chalets, import game for hunting, and build a nine-hole golf course, marketed at an overseas clientele. This, of course, meant that there would no longer be any need for farm workers. They therefore respectfully included severance packages (of a more than compensatory amount), and requested the workers to leave before the end of the month, otherwise legal action would be taken.

Standing outside their small cottages, showing their letters to one another, they read the same words over and over. They did not speak anymore. They did not cry. Instead they turned and looked at their cottages, their small gardens and washing lines. Behind their homes, in the distance, they saw the cemetery; grey gravestones neatly spaced, surrounded by a low wall of white. A marker of those they had lost; the old, the young, the stillborn; it had formed the background to their lives. What would happen, they wondered, to the dead? Who would tend to them once the living had left?

Isaac Witbooi stood to one side, away from the others. His grief was his own. His grandparents, parents, siblings, wife and children had all been buried in that earth, leaving him with no one. He carried silently the loneliness of years. Aging now, perhaps sixty, perhaps more, he had come to look forward with certainty to the day he would join his family in the cemetery. Robbed of that possibility, Isaac Witbooi looked to the future as an empty plain without end. There was no horizon; only stretching out, flat and dim, the years to come.

In the week that followed, Isaac went to neighbouring farms, asking for jobs from people he had known for years. He did not beg or plead, nor did he remind them of the past when he had given advice or the sweat of his brow in times of need. Instead, he anticipated their words, knowing full well what they would say:

"You were always a good worker, but you're an old man now. What can we give you to do?"

As the end of the month neared, Isaac packed his belongings into a brown cardboard suitcase which had belonged to his wife. Over the years of disuse its fastening had rusted so that he had to tie a length of rope around it in order to keep it closed. The few items inside – clothes, razor, bible, mug, plates and cutlery – rattled against each other as he lifted it. Glancing around the small cottage to see if he had everything, Isaac then stepped outside, and closed the door behind him, before removing the key from the lock and pushing it under the door as they had been asked to do.

Among the last to leave, Isaac said goodbye to nobody. Those who remained stayed only out of a reckless hope that the end of the month would never come, or if it did that something miraculous would happen to prevent their eviction. Unwilling to see the desperate looks on their faces, Isaac said nothing, feeling only their eyes on him from behind the windows of their cottages as he passed by. He felt no remorse for parting from these people he had known since their births, for it was, after all, not them that he was abandoning. Instead it was the cemetery that he was leaving, and with it all the years of his life, and those of his parents' and his grandparents' lives too. They were years he could not put a number to, nothing exact, because each year held so much of every other. Whether a hundred, or whether less or more, those years made up his past, and with every step he took, the suitcase banging against his thigh, it was as though a moment of that past was beaten out of him.

All morning he walked, passing families he recognized who had made camp on the side of the road.

"Sit, have a rest, Oupa," they greeted him, sipping tea boiled over small fires.

Isaac shook his head, pressed on.

"What's the rush?" they called after him. "There's no work that way! You're walking to nothing!"

By the time he approached his destination; a large service station with a restaurant and café; his ears were ringing with fatigue. He felt dizzy – from the walk, from thirst, from age, and from the weight of the suitcase, heavy and awkward at his side. Dizziness settled in his throat as he approached the intersection beside the service station. Already the roadside was crowded with workers who had left the farm a day, a week, before. They greeted him with wariness, silently making a space for him beside them. As he put down his suitcase, sitting upon it like a chair, they asked whom he had seen, what news he had. But Isaac had nothing to share, and soon they tired of him, returning to standing with their hands in their pockets, frowning up and down the intersection, waiting for something that wouldn't come.

From where he sat, Isaac looked back towards the large area taken up by the service station. Among the uniform-clad petrol attendants he recognized Randall, a young man he had taken under his wing a few years previously, teaching him all he knew about farming and maintenance of vines. Further away, near the doorway to the toilets, Isaac could make out Randall's wife and sister carrying mops and buckets. They, too, were in the service station's uniform; bright colours covering them from head to toe. Keeping their faces low, their eyes on the ground, neither Randall nor the women allowed themselves to look up towards where their friends and family sat beside the road, their belongings scattered around them. Even from a distance, Isaac understood by their expressions the guilt they felt for their fortune. He turned around, facing the road so that his shame need not become theirs.

For five days Isaac remained, as men younger than himself were picked up on the backs of farm bakkies, either for jobs or simply hitching rides to anywhere else. By the afternoon of the third day he no longer joined the other men as they crowded around the windows of stopping cars, murmuring qualifications. The drivers took in his old and lined face, his trembling hands and watery eyes and shook their heads. They had no work for him. He should go home, they said. He was too old to be hired. It was time for him to rest, to have his children take care of him. Isaac stepped back from the rolled-down car windows, allowing others to take his place in the crowd.

On the sixth day Isaac woke alone in the damp grass beside the road. The last few men and women had left the previous afternoon, wandering off in the direction of other towns or back towards the farm, hoping to get work from the developers. He picked up his suitcase, and without eating, without wiping the sleep from his eyes, Isaac began to walk. For that whole day, and the day to follow, Isaac was still familiar with his surroundings. Many times he had passed these lands during windy rides on the back of the old farmer's bakkie. Going slower now, Isaac could pay more attention to the view - the length of the grass beside the road, items of litter, the mountains both nearby and distant. Yet the stillness of the air surprised him, its closeness around him, and he had to pause from time to time to sit on his suitcase and rest. What was more, slowed down by traveling on foot, Isaac now passed the carcasses of animals crushed by cars and was able to identify them. Innards, feathers and fur separated out from what had been a mass, into dreadful detail. What had been nameless was now recognizable as crow, porcupine, snake.

He ate when he could, using the severance money sparingly. But days often passed between roadside cafes and he was driven to scavenge. For two days he ate nothing but fallen oranges, picked up through a hole in an orchard fence. His stomach cramped in pain, his body began to leak, so that he was forced for a day and a night to lie in a ditch, wet with sweat and shit, unable to move.

With time, Isaac became aware of an increase in traffic, of less vegetation, of the steep terrain flattening out. The road kill altered too. Dogs now, and cats, lay bloating in the sun. He stepped around them, careful not to disturb the flies. Beside the body of a medium-sized dog, its hind legs crooked and bleeding, he paused. It was still breathing; panting heavily. There was nothing he could give it; he had no water, nothing for the pain. Isaac bent down to pat it on the head and it twitched its tail limply in response. When it began to whine he quickly continued on his way.

In the distance nothing was clear. There was only a shadow, dark, spreading out over the flatlands, brown and dreadful. Soon people began to appear, laden as he was, with bags, with firewood, buckets of water on their heads. They passed him, moving away from the road into a thick island of shacks. Children played nearby, jumping over a burning tyre, splashing in a puddle of sewerage water from which goats were drinking. Isaac stopped. He felt tired now. Very tired. He sat down on the suitcase and put his head in his hands. When night fell, Isaac stayed where he was. Above him, the sky held no stars. There was only the darkness and the sounds of cars, of gunshots, screaming, laughing.

He woke in the morning to a sky quivering and pink. A woman was passing nearby carrying water, and he called to her softly.

"Tatamkhulu, are you lost?" She asked as he drank from the container with his hands. He did not answer.

"Tatamkhulu, you can't sleep here on the side of the road. It's dangerous."

"There?" he asked, pointing at the shacks.

"Yes, you can build a home there. If you wait long enough, maybe ten years, then maybe you will get a proper house from the government."

"And the dead?" he asked. "Where do you bury the dead?"

She shook her head, "Not here. We take them home. We bury them back where they came from."

"And if there is no one to take them back? No place to go back to?"

"The government," she said. "They take them away. I don't know. Maybe they burn them. Maybe they bury them. I don't know. We take our people back so I don't know."

Isaac thanked her for the water and got up, lifting his suitcase.

"You must go to your family, Tatamkhulu," the woman said. "You mustn't stay here."

Isaac nodded. He would not stay here. Not in a place so foreign, not a place which held nothing in which he could recognize himself. He did not know where he would go. Only back, that was what he knew. He would go back.

Several hours later Isaac passed the dog he had seen the previous day. It was still panting beside the road, its mouth dry and heavy. He watched the steady rush of passing cars. No one had stopped for the dog. It would die where it lay. Continuing slowly on his way, surrounded by the roar of traffic, Isaac understood that those who died alone belonged to nobody. Their bones were dust, their names unspoken.

Am my own man

by Deon Simphiwe Skade

I can hear her voice wail
like an impatient church bell
it echoes in stately shrills

lack of restraint
casts her into the darkness of fears
"Be a man! Be a man, Joe!" she had demanded of me
as if she knew what she meant
as if she herself was a man
but since I had studied her ways,
her innermost self
i had run away from her demands
her command of things she knew nothing about

i have been on the run since then
running towards becoming my own man
and when the bell rings now
i discover a new form of cynicism towards stately things

POEMS FROM BELHAR HIGH SCHOOL, CAPE TOWN

Die vuur op vygieskraal
by Tanya Booysen

my mooi pop is weg
in die brand
net die hare bly oor
in die sand
ek was te haastig veroggend op skool toe
en het nie my gewoone goodbye gese nie

my pop is net soe oud soos ek
"n present van my oorlede ouma
eenvoudige
goedkoop
plastieke
speelding
ek gaan jou mis.

The shop
by Shandre Cupido

My mom works at a fish shop in claremont
i go there after school with my sister sometimes
and i see how hard she works
with sweat pouring from her face amongst the heat and the oil
sometimes during her break
we will go walking in claremont gardens
sit on the benches
and throw chips for the pigeons
and we will hug each other
then she goes back to the heat and oil

Die klein begin'
by Kevin Dyssel

Elke Sondag na kerk gaan my ma en ek
my oudste broer in Polsmoor besoek
ek is baie lief vir my broer
en is baie excited om hom te sien
dan kan ons lekker oor die rugby praat
en will hom van die goeie nuus vertel
dat ons a brief gekry het
ons gaan a huis in die Delft kry
hy gaan so bly wees
ons eerste huis
ek kan nie wag nie

A view of Delft
(Written during the battle for Symphony Way 2008)
by Andre Marais

From my classroom window 2nd floor 3rd period
dense black smoke ladders
to the sky from a distance
remnants of a battle scene close by
as the city bares its teeth
declares war on the poor
implements the letter of yet another court order
from faraway Cape town
against those who dared to be audacious
who will not wait "their turn"
who dares to bite the hand that feeds them
refusing to fit the role of the 'deserving poor'

Rainbow nation ubuntu is on the roll here
as police kick open makeshift doors
to half incomplete matchbox houses
wrestle down frail malnutrioned women
and pregnant teeage girls give birth on the pavement
fist clenched   climbing to sun
openly declaring their determination to fightback
and pensioners die in the sand

the careless machismo of the offcial reportage about hysterical women
miss the malignant lump when party politics goes recruiting in Deftland

Extract From 'Emzana Shack Recollections'

by L. Sojini

In case you didn't know, this fella is too young to go politicking, so if I don't wanna end in solitary confinement with a treason charge, I gotta keep my mouth glued. Presidential amnesty is a rarity in these circles. Tamkhulu always says 'life is all about politics, relationships and money.' I know his heart lightens up when I enquire how they used to do things back in the days.

He claims the somebodies owned the finer things when he and his people scrambled for the bit they had, fighting for the land belonging to their forefathers. I hate it when he says young people of today get it all good. Why then don't we live in 'Surbs'?

Never mind! I like it here.

If Tamkhulu and his people fought against the somebodies, why does he and I and the rest of these somebodies with their families still squat in places like these? He thinks I'm too young to understand. Next time I will ask him to go fight again – maybe we can really win this time – rather than only having useless points displayed on the board (black one!). How can he have the audacity to claim that young people of today get it all good when I just ran past Mancane's spaza shop? He has to think again, that gwinya should have found its way in my stomach.

Who says I also don't wanna be a big bellied somebody?

Only kidding!

I hope there is nothing wrong in trying to gain a few kilos. I'll tell you a secret: I think I have these somebodies, feasting on what I take in, maybe that's the reason why I stay thin like a pin. I know many girls dream of my body, especially models. Slenderness is an obsession – of course it's the ads on TV. Diet and stuff, pills and stuff, exercise and stuff, mirrors and stuff – man! I wonder why I actually waste my emotions feeling for them. They struggle for a body that I so wish to discard. Maybe these somebodies and I should trade places. That means I can even try modelling then I can scream in Tamkhulu's face that yes, young fellas we get it all good. But then my ribs will transparently say hello to everyone who has the time to greet back.

Mandilakhe says he no longer goes for Mancane's gwinyas, serious allegations this laaitie got. 'She wipes her daughters bum and without washing them she prepares gwinyas for the whole nation.' Yuck! That's crazy. Somebody school these mothers about hygiene and please remind me who the minister of health is. Is it still Mantombazana? The beetroot stuff – it's only the media trying to cash in on my main man. I miss you doggess, where the hell you at? I know I'm behind time – it's not my fault but Tamkhulu's, because he buys the previous week's dispatch – saying it's half the original price.

Mandi, don't fool these somebodies reading this book – I know you like those gwinyas – like me, you just don't have the money. I'm warning you not to go around spreading propaganda. You never know in these time we living in – you might get sued for defamation of character. I hope these somebodies won't go ahead cause a somebody like you got nothing to offer – they only will be wasting their money – and trust me you don't have millions of taxpayers money to cover your legal woes. Mandi, my friend, don't mind me calling you a nobody but referring you as a somebody is too good for your own liking.

Alright Tamkhulu, you also say life is about relationships.

Somebody, if you still reading this, just know I'm still running on my two going somewhere. I'll tell you in a while.

Talk about relationships – if the one that you Tamkhulu have with Makhulu is something to go by then . . . let me keep my big mouth shut because I was just about to ask about what happens to those who can't control their things – maybe they must be shot and killed – but then I can't lose my grandfather because of love matters.

'Getting along with some people, is what I mean when I'm talking about relationships,' that's the sound of Tamkhulu never ending melody. I always make him repeat his statements so he can confirm his say. Is not getting along with someone not a relationship? I try putting him in a corner. 'Get it all good young fella,' he addresses me like a youth that I am. 'Think of a workplace, if you don't get along with your colleague somebodies, it means you just having a sour relationship and that is part of life – you can't always get it all good like kids of nowadays – it's a problem crumpling isizwe esimnyama, they got it all bad.' Tamkhulu has a habit of messing my rather already messed up day. If he earlier sounded melodic now in a space of a millisecond he has changed in time to come across as tralodic! What? I just created a new word – tralody, tralodic. Please put me in the Guinness or in the dictionary.

Stiff! Think about relationships, Bess, Banda and the rest of these somebodies always take our ball when we play soccer down the road. How can I forget that Sizo somebody – should have been a father than a lazy student. Worse of all, he preys on young boys for their lunchboxes and never forgets to empty your pockets to coin a couple of dirty pieces you even don't have to afford a smoke that he and his Buntu friend share in the toilet at break time – that's if he is even in a good mood to come and stay that long to watch the hours if not decades pass at school. The teachers have a neck of applauding him – that's their way of telling us direct and vehemently in our faces that coming to school everyday no matter the rain or what, what is all in vain. I guess we give it to them all too good. I'm on the verge of finalising an amendment that will allow me to cut my attendance probably in half. Maybe these somebodies will know that it takes effort, tears and blood to be present at school. All they find pleasurable than teaching is beating us for sweet mahala when we come to school late or don't know the answers to their conundrums they couldn't even dare answering to their university lecturers. Sizo and these somebodies paint a picture of a bitter two-way combo. I hate how they celebrate him and his Buntu friend. Deep down I get the feeling that these teacher somebodies are at ease when these good fellas are on 'holiday'. The time they love school is when they are on the run from the police than being told to write the whole day at school – they and their police buddies must be bold and jump out of the closet cause I see no reason why they chase each other around like headless chickens. Come on! Who the hell are you trying to fool, pretending like they don't love each other? They rather be romancing each other at an exotic place in hell than think we kids.

Tamkhulu speaks of certain relationships gone sour. Tralodies sang by most somebodies go like 'when you wanted your high positions, you came to the people and we promised you votes but after that you go away forgetting about us.' This infamous tralody sounds familiar right? I won't talk about the ministerial handbook just for the heck of it because its relationship time not political corner! Anyway you receive your grant and they never bother if you squander it on booze, so it's fair that we give them space – they have a right to travel first class, throw ostentatious parties – they too have rights and to put cherry on top, they work hard and deserve whatever their hands can find themselves with. At least they provide computers with LCD screens to rural schools and these kids don't have to cough up any cash – if you don't believe me, look for a school called Lengeni. It's in Ndabakazi, Butterworth, Transkei.

Somebody tell me who the president is, is it still Bra t Bo touch Mbeki? We miss you man. Don't blame me for being a get it all good fella. The only time I ever have some dirty coins in my cream turned black pocket is when my Tamkhulu bribes me (well the other pockets have Kimberley holes in them). He claims to love only my granny but then he forgets that sometimes. Don't ask me how I know but he scores more than you and more than you can possibly ever dream. Every time he goes on the rampage I kinda feel like I'm on the receiving end – I guess that's how I get to bust his ass up! Pity Makhulu does not have this special instinct. I wouldn't go around bragging about it. As Tamkhulu always put it, no matter how pathetic it sounds I have to listen attentively. 'You get it all good, young fellas are actually women disguised as men!' Of course I'm sensitive but feminine is another issue for another day. Gays? I don't see them around, only on TV.

He has to give me something, otherwise if I tell granny he'll have to consider sleeping in the warmth of the cold outside. What he doesn't realise is that he's more feminine than I am. But in everything I do refrain from convincing him that he's more feminine than I. But I would kill myself if I found out that my Tamkhulu is a g . . . . Many are times I feel guilty of pressing the panic button for Makhulu is more of a man than we – Tamkhulu and I – she got balls of steel! Money talk – he is at his most alarming state of sensitivity. He pretends like he despises it. Then why does the nails on his head crumple when his sons and daughters purposely forgets to send him some of the good stuff to punish him for their rough upbringing? No matter what the case in the highest court of the land is, you can't change your parents so they are entitled to think twice and you'll see an ear to ear smile on his face. What about the grant money? He goes to the shebeen to wine on makambas with his cronies. Different loony characters frequent the shebeen. In case I didn't tell you, around here we speak Xhosa but this other day I heard this dude speak Sotho saying 'Hawu Transkei, mo and a ke robali.' Well, I know I should be writing this book in Xhosa – don't kill me – I'll get it translated if the manuscript is complete. But who will publish junk!? From short somebodies who totter when walking even not drunk to tall somebodies in brown overalls and the big bellied devils, Mzana – thanks to the shebeen is a mixed bag.

As for Sizo and his Buntu friend – you know where they will graduate! – I don't have to tell you that, do I? Money is a sensitive issue just like sex. Many people vainly shun away from it. But can you ever run away from life? Death is the only hiding. So when Tamkhulu tries to dismiss money-talk, I know he might be drunk or not ready to part some dirty pieces after being busted. 'It is love that makes the world go round,' is a melody that alludes 'it is money that makes the world go round' to sound like a tralody.

Okay, run, stop! I have been running ever since and now let me stop. But before I take a breather – running along the crooked paths of Emzana, resembling those of a maze designed by a lazy overpaid, under working, disrespectful town planner – I accidentally bump into somebody. Drumming him in his stomach with my right shoulder. Helplessly

I watched on as his eyes almost popped off his sockets direct onto the dusty ground. Anxiously waiting for his not-so-many teeth also to jump off the refuse truck – all I hear as he opens his sorry excuse of a mouth are whimpers of grown man groaning in torment infiltrating the atmospheric pressure. Judging by the two teeth left in the old man's mouth – if my math is spot on – it's obvious, the dog won't bite, in spite such fury. His hands held me by the collar of my worn out tee shirt. No chance of letting myself loose availed as he tightened his grip on my neck – prohibiting the air that had brought me crashing into him. Sad part – I could fidget all I wanted – but trust me – no way out. His sweaty palms oiled my parched neck. Spats of saliva stimulated by his wrath came gushing out – somebody had opened the gates of hell! With my mind racing my other eye managed to notice the wire that fastened his grey trousers from falling. The sweaty palms no longer caressed me but made breathing a luxury I could only hope for. Everybody – and I say everybody – I mean all the Zanas started flocking around to see the action – first hand – gossip in this area takes second place. Everyone had to see with own eyes otherwise your tale would be classified under fiction. In full view of these somebodies the old man dragged me like a trash can refusing to enter the trash truck to an old open space that used to be an incinerator until somebody from Copenhagen sent a letter to warn us from polluting the air we breathe. Trust me if you come next week, the place will be housing new shacks. Instead of helping the young chap out they cheered on the one minute devil (probably graduating after reading 'Hell For Dummies') to teach me a lesson. Talk about community ills. From their faces you could sense boredom and through my misery and thrashing I was a mere object of entertainment to these somebodies. At least I deserved dirty coins thrown onto the centre stage for providing something worthwhile in their sad lives – in the process involuntarily sacrificing my blood to be spilled.

Of course I was preparing to go through the fire but still nervous I was. I wonder why he delayed in getting this over with. Maybe he waited upon all the somebodies to show up so they would crown him hero then after that he could end his sorrowful life and die a happy man. The more I looked to the sky as well in the crowd for help I saw no-one I could pin my hopes of escaping alive. If I counted on getting loose miraculously for sure there had to be divine intervention in the play. As for me I could not match the old man's strength that he required to dismantle the skinny boy in me.

Something tells me I have seen this man before. In fact, Tamkhulu had shown him to me. Although he told me after some time why they were on each other's throats I sensed tension between the two from the word go. To put it raw – they hated each other – and today I can't help but feel that this whole tsunami is not all about me, just the old man sending a red signal to Tamkhulu. My Tamkhulu – I will stand for no matter what. Loyalty is what he always preach. You must be curious to know why the two old men didn't see eye to eye. The other day at a local shebeen while Tamkhulu was on the rampage with a certain lady he declined to mention even when I made a deal that next time I catch him in the act, I would keep mum and choose not to reveal my findings to granny. He came back to find his beer gone – only the empty bottle remaining. If he had known that beer would cause such rift he would have took it with him. But I guess he had a serious case to attend behind closed doors. In life, Tamkhulu adores only his two lalas's – his lager and of course his ladies that always put him in deep trouble with granny. To make matters worse the old man threatened to expose him of his secret affairs if he didn't buy him another kamba. Talk about opportunists of all kind. This angered Tamkhulu – taking his last money and having to watch somebody drink his money. Well if you threaten my TK, sure case I will hunt after your skeleton. Who does he think he is anyway? I am the only one with a right embedded in the South African constitution allowing me to manipulate Tamkhulu off his pennies. From that day Tamkhulu had a grudge, he wanted to break his neck there and there but his lady companion advised him not to. He knew the day would come and if it never did Tamkhulu was sure to resume the farce in hell. Unfortunately it was not this day. A golden chance passed him. What I love about Tamkhulu is that he shares things with me so that I can be a better somebody tomorrow. Before he actually tells me I kinda sense them so he has no option but confide in me. It's funny that he is wary of granny whereas when it comes to his peers or foes alike he is ready to crack their skulls out of their heads. I guess he has two sides to him. Not the sensitive and feminine softie I thought him to be. 'A man's gotta do what a man's gotta do,' he likes to say. Yippee my Tamkhulu is not g .... Wherever he got that 'man gotta do' stuff I don't give a ... , but I have a problem with that somebody who taught him that.

The bongo man's ring tone at dawn
by Jethro Louw

The bongo man's ring tone at dawn
Walks on into the lyrics of a song
It's dancing around a stone clock tower
Inspiration lights up his fire
For years it was dry here
And we kept on searching for that elusive rain dear

Many tribes man
Them they has stepped into the stride of the trance
Them they took a glance
Into that
That was once
In a dance
My tribes man dance

The bongo man's ring tone
It's the blues from the bosom of Abraham
Distress in the roots of Ham
Reunited a rock band
Across the borders of clan
Unified the tribal jam
That fans and fuels the roots of dread
The San in a circle when the herbs man breaks there bread
On the songs of the red rolling dunes
Melodies from the grasslands
Click to the chants from the valley of the sun
It's the rhythms that we dance to in the Hantam
The tribes man
The tribes man of my clan

The lyrics of Tanneman /Xam - The Plakkerskamp Poet

Are the dogs perhaps in charge?

by Len Verwey

The shelters will not stand a storm
still they build them packed together
on any slope of land. Women take hours
shaping clay and sand canals
between the corrugated iron walls
and the driftwood fences,
which the grey-brown torrent,
when it builds again from distance,
will disregard entirely
and flood again the earth floors and the pathetic
furniture and possessions.

They'll gather around to inspect the damage,
then begin to drain the rooms
and re-shape the canals.
 On the angled banks of the stream
the roots of trees protrude
like veins on a tourniqueted arm.

And though there is flooding
the women still must queue
for water at the trickling standpipes
with their jugs and buckets,
empty 2 litre plastic bottles,
any receptacle they can find and
drag and push and roll to where they live.

Half or more of the water routed here,
from the dam that lies up beside
the mountain pass up there,
lost along the way through creaking pipes
and farm diversions and all the other
rusted infrastructure
money is always hard to find for.

This is not our problem.
But what reaches here,
dehydration, tb, malnutrition, cholera
and hiv might become so. And can it be here,
as the generals say,
that marauder leaders lurk?

Are the dogs perhaps in charge?
Or the big-eyed children lined
against the wall who kick a gutted ball
as soon as we depart?

Their chalk-ringed games could be a
form of code, as could the graffiti
on every open piece of concrete,
the phone numbers in the station toilet,
the unread patient records
at the aspirin-for-everything clinic,
surely too the words
of the minister in the clearing
where the mothers gather
for their prayer and penance.

Sunday afternoon. Between rains.
Near your coastal city.
All would be bearable, today as every day,
if it weren't for the constant singing.

TWO POEMS
by Raeez Jacobs

The Anthropologist

Johannesburg – I, the novelist clutch my notepad
I, the exhibitionist, exhibit the norm –
Hot coffee at Arts on Main-
I'm an artist, deliberately painting my face
To gel in with the African risqué.
Others watch me while I watch them
We're all busy;
Immersed in our own lives . . .
I could have mistaken the dark for the light
It's all multifarious
A few fro's passed me by
Along with some men in blue overalls-
They represent the streets,
The nakedness of every foot
And the leaves on every tree
I, the Anthropologist, dissect stigmas,
Maybe it's not true that all people in shawls
Are fine artists
Or that that boy in broken All-Stars plays the guitar
Nelson Mandela's statue could not represent them all,
In Johannesburg they are more than diverse.

Perfection

It's never easy resisting the urge to be beautiful,
Your face wanting to be the whisper of the ocean
And your hair the strands of the golden bay

You long for a Tuscan sunrise
A mellifluous crack of dawn,
You want your hands to be piano-smooth
And your back to be mountain steady

We're never pleased,
We want to be tasteful to the lips of another
Soothing to the hands of some other
And we warp our faces in the crowd
And straighten our hairs
As if they're Christmas curtains

We coat our lungs with the finest tar,
Inhaling the urge to cry
Hoping the mirror doesn't lie.

The Martyrdom of Father Gonzalo da Silveria

by Msiki Tagamuchira Mziki

Fr. Gonzalo da Silveria was a very disappointed man. On graduating from the Jesuit College at Lisbon, he had wasted no time in submitting his name for a mission to Goa or Africa to convert savages to the Christian faith. He was a man absolutely subdued by his religious convictions and understood the urgency with which the Gospel needed to be spread to the four corners of the earth. According to him, in an age when Vasco Da Gama had brought immeasurable wealth to his monarch by opening a trade route to India, and Magellan had circumnavigated the earth, spreading the good news was the only worthwhile thing left to be done. Like most educable Jesuits, he was beginning to be won over to the most unlikely theory that the world was round. Of course, it was ridiculous, but men had set off eastwards and arrived from the west; honourable men whose word could be relied upon entirely. And in his travels round the Cape towards the East African coast, he could not help but notice the rotund aspect lent to the world by the ever-shifting horizon. He still believed that the earth, sun and moon all moved in one great circle at the behest of the Almighty. The new doctrines in mathematics and natural philosophy considerably interested Gonzalo da Silveira and not a few of his Jesuit colleagues regarded him as a half-wit, an eccentric and an upstart. He dismissed all of them with a twirl of the lip and a shrug of the shoulder. His dedication to the faith was greatly intensified by the infamous break from the Church by Luther and Calvin. He considered it the duty of every recipient of the sacrament of baptism to defend the Catholic Church with their very souls if need be.

Gonzalo da Silveira was not a poor man. Indeed, his family was considered by their peers to be more than comfortable and his father was not without connections at the King's court. An astute man of the world, his father had recognized at the very onset the great opportunities occasioned by the trade in silk and spices. He had become in a decade, perhaps the biggest distributor and depository of both commodities in Portugal. Gold and silver were much more difficult to come by, but like all industrious men, he   compelled nature to yield to his will and, through a constant effort, became an important merchant in precious metals throughout Christendom. This existence of a mercantile interest in the Silveira family was not the handiwork of Gonzalo's father alone. His great grandfather had become affluent by trading with the Genovese and had amassed considerable wealth by selling food and armaments to the Christian armies at the time of the last crusade. Therefore, in embracing the Christian faith with all the power of his consciousness, Gonzalo was only giving back to the faith what his ancestors had rightfully taken from it. He held himself with the total poise and bearing of one to who even the Creator was beholden. After all, there were only three honourable vocations for a man: the cloth, the sea and troth. He amused himself with the very true reflection that, by coming to East Africa, he had had beneficially combined the first two.

His first disappointment with Africa had been the total absence of savages. He had always imagined himself landing on a pristine African shore and mooring his pathetic craft to a mighty banyan. Confronting him in one mass, like an impenetrable green wall, he had expected a solid tropical forest so dense that the eye could not penetrate a few inches. He had expected to reach the great kingdom in the interior that he was headed for at the paltry progress of one mile a day; his skin freckled and mottled with the scratches of all sorts of thorns and the varied stings of a myriad insects. He felt particularly proud of himself because he expected to die of pox or fevers before he reached his destination, or be bitten by a serpent or mauled by a lion. Gonzalo da Silveira had set off for Africa with a heart full of kindness for the entire human race - and why not, since he considered himself already sacrificed.

In the event, his passage was peaceful to the very point of tediousness. They had enjoyed a calm and friendly sea all the way and had not had the opportunity to be even mildly seasick. On arrival at the coast, he had been very upset by the sight of a fairly passable harbour with three Arab dhows at anchor. A horde of dark black men rowed out to them in a small boat and, after greeting the captain in tones of unmistakable familiarity delivered in fluent Portuguese, proceeded with the business of unloading the cargo and taking it ashore. It was explained, while he listened with a sinking heart, that they were actually paid for this service. He was horrified that these people had a notion of money.

At this same coast, Fr Silveira was fortunate to secure the services of a man who would serve him well throughout his stay in Africa. He was a black giant named Tete whose command of Portuguese had been cultivated by previous encounters with the White Man. Among his other attributes were a ready smile and an honest face.

The trip from the seashore to the kingdom in the interior was no more eventful than the maritime voyage. The trail had been blazed by Mohammedan traders centuries before and, traveling up the great Save River, Gonzalo da Silveira lost all hope of adventure. The river was a fair enough freeway and now required only the efforts of a few slaves to render it fully navigable. He was even more disappointed that, although they came across several wild beasts including numerous snakes and six lions, they were all remarkable for the speed with which they made themselves scarce. Only the mosquitoes and the infernal heat managed to bother the Jesuit a little, and he wished to be bothered.

When their party made camp each night on a dry nook in the swampy flood plain of the Save, he could hardly sleep a wink. The mosquitoes made an intolerable racket and the ground was never really dry from the almost incessant rain. It rained in Africa almost out of the blue sky and when the wind was not driving too strongly, his company advised him to trek on in the rain in order to reach the kingdom on time.

There was no end to the disappointment of Gonzalo da Silveira. Within a week of his arrival at the court of the great Munhumutapa, His Majesty, King Mapunza Gutu himself acquiesced to the entreaties of a great faith and, together with his wives and children, was duly baptized. He appeared desperate to escape the lure of his other visitors who sought to convert him to Islam. He could not distinguish their religion from their trade interests and for that reason associated it with treachery. He was also intimidated by the strict edicts of Islam, which appeared to him harsh and punitive. Christianity itself sounded as if it had its fair share of horrors and sadism, but there were aspects to it that took his breath away and a romance that often left him in tears. This new faith never sought to know where he kept his gold, a matter that appeared central to the vocation of the Arabs.

In spite of a thrilling heart, Fr Silveira was somewhat dismayed to find the king so understanding. The linguistic talents of Tete also meant that their communications were efficient and mutually fulfilling. The king therefore, wasted no time in grasping the importance of becoming a subject of the great King of Portugal – soon to be Emperor-, the greatest nation in the Christian Diaspora, and exhorted the missionary to urgently secure that prize for him.

The king was as wise as he was charming and well mannered, possessing the carriage of one quite used to ruling over men and deciding important matters. His was a very fair complexion and the features of his face were pleasant and kindly. His limbs were straight and his body solid. In another place and with another colour, Fr Silveira considered that Mapunza Gutu could have been thought of as a very handsome man.

His women were good. The Munhumutapa had five wives at his court and Fr Silveira wondered how many others elsewhere. The man apparently had an infinite capacity for marriage. The oldest of his wives was a great deal older than the king himself and the priest was given to understand that the king had inherited her, childless, from his late father. The toll of a difficult life and frequent childbirth made it difficult to judge an African woman's age, but Fr Silveira guessed that at nearly sixty, she was a good twenty years older than Mapunza Gutu and could easily have passed for the grandmother of his youngest wife who was pregnant at fourteen. In spite of crude cuts to their faces (a bizarre form of make-up), bare breasts and unkempt kinks of hair, there remained about them all a certain royal serenity. The youngest three still possessed the comeliness of youth and, when wrapped exquisitely in the colourful linen presented them by various Arab traders, were very clearly a credit to the king. Goncalo da Silveira knew that his appreciation of them was necessarily limited by the novelty of their colour but could guess from the glint of satisfaction lingering in the king's eyes that they were exceptionally beautiful people.

Fr Silveira did not covet pretty women. It was all very well to appreciate in its fullness the beauty of God's creation, and Woman was the pinnacle of that beauty. The Garden of Eden, tranquil with brooks, lush with shrubs and fragrant with flowers, was still incidental to the Woman. Being fully aware of this, Fr Silveira had yet rejected the idea of making a career of any woman. At the age of sixteen, he had entered the seminary at Lisbon determined to live a life of complete chastity and, finding it easier than he had expected, was able to take a serious vow of celibacy at age seventeen. That he had not in his life permitted himself carnal knowledge of a woman was with him a point of honour for, at least in that one respect, he was equal to Christ.

But it must not be thought that his life had lacked in temptations. His noble mother had been very determined to get a grandson out of him and had no patience with the priesthood. She had a fair respect for religion but was amply supported by scripture in her postulation that a man could serve God with equal devotion whatever his marital status. As it was the duty of every man to provide for his children, it was also his duty to supply offspring to inherit his wealth. Her influence in Iberia was not inconsiderable and she relentlessly flung a series of delectable maidens at her son from the respectable houses of Spain and Portugal. That her son had taken a vow to God and was undertaking difficult training was the least of her concerns and Gonzalo had to contend with a fortnightly invitation to his mother's house for yet another introduction. However, all her efforts were in vain.

*

After a month at the Mutapa capital city, Danamombe, Fr Silveira's work was finished. The conversion of their king to the new faith had seemingly convinced all the pagans to accept Christ. Fr Silveira did not know by sight any man in the kingdom who was not a Christian and he was actively contemplating traveling southwards to convert the warlike tribes there settled. Of course, there still remained among the Karanga a sprinkling of heathen belief and customs. Fr Silveira appreciated that not even such a great religion as Christianity could, in an instant, wipe away practices observed over many centuries. Indeed, the greatest opposition to his teaching came from the Arab traders who had settled at Danamombe - and who were not without influence with the king.

The head of their mission was a small pot-bellied man named Ahmed; he had a swarthy complexion and a beard hanging well below his navel. Ahmed made it quite clear that the Jesuit priest was an unwelcome interferer and did his best to ignore him. Being himself descended from a line of tradesmen, he could not dispel the suspicion that Fr Silveira was fronting religion for the purposes of commerce. Ahmed had tried to introduce his religion to the Karanga but they evidently had no stamina for it. It is difficult to motivate superstitious and animist savages to pray to an unaccustomed god five times a day. So he had given it up as useless; trying to bribe Tete to lure the missionary away also failed. In the end, however, he was forced to accept that the priest was a harmless fool with absolutely no notion of commerce. On this basis he settled down to enjoy himself at the king's court, practicing considerable lewdness and gathering as much gold as he could for his family at Abu Dhabi.

Perhaps the only person whose opposition to the Christian influence never wavered was Jenaguru, the king's youngest sister. She was eighteen years old and betrothed to the king himself. This inbreeding appalled the Jesuit but Tete explained that thus was obtained an heir of full royal blood. Gonzalo da Silveira still considered the arrangement incestuous, an affront to God and a travesty of human fellowship. So he looked upon Jenaguru who was also a spirit medium as the author of a scandal and took her refusal to accept Christianity as a compliment to God and a favour to himself.

As it was, he was starting to be tire of people and needed something, or someone, to hate without contrition. To wake up each morning and reflect that the nearest kingdom of white men was six thousand miles away was unbearable and the sight, chatter, manner and odour of the blacks were more than flesh and blood could bear. He was particularly incensed that that his hosts surmised that they were of equal standing to him; some even flung at him the superciliousness reserved for the despicable 'intruder'. Fr Silveira's good spirits ebbed, his heart sank. The various delicacies foisted on him by the king's kind wives failed to arouse his appetite; his skin traded its healthy glow for a sickening pallor. Then his nerves failed and his bowel lost its rhythm. It was only to be expected that at this point Fr Goncalo da Silveira sincerely wished he had never set sail from Lisbon.

But a very curious event restored the pastor's waning interest in his flock. He set out alone one sunny morning to fish for the abundant bream in one of the sparkling streams near Danamombe. Even after a long and lonely stay in Africa, the beauty of the land still took a man's breath away. It was pure, wholesome and unadulterated. The true charm of savages is that they know not even how to pollute. The pastures were rich and endless, the beasts happy and healthy. All land belonged to the monarch and cultivation was limited. It was possible to set one's foot down in the pleasant knowledge that no other human being had done the same in that very spot since creation. Human settlements were but mere dots in the middle of jungles where ruled only beasts, snakes and insects.. Fr Silveira could not withhold a wispy smile as he set his reed trap expertly against some smooth rocks and laughed aloud with pleasure as a sizeable fish leapt over the rocks, straight into his basket. One more followed, and then another. He was about to reset the trap when the play of light on the water alerted him that he had company. Believing it was a wild beast come to drink, he froze instinctively and furtively scoured the vicinity with wary eyes. Then he saw her.

At a large pool about fifty yards distant, where a bend in the river and some bushes almost hid her from view, a girl was bathing in the stream. Her melodious voice at that instant reached his ears and he could tell that she swam with pure pleasure. She heaved herself onto a boulder and lay down to dry in the sun. Just as suddenly, she turned her head and he was met with a piercing stare. It was Jenaguru. Still looking at him, she leapt back into the water, submerging her nude vitals.

Something quite unthinkable then happened to Fr Silveira. His blood warmed up rapidly and his cheeks hardened with emotion. There was an unfamiliar flutter in his heart, which rendered him breathless. He felt his manhood firmly assert itself and was ashamed to stand up straight.

Without further ado, he threw his catch into the basket and stomped off home. There, he proceeded straight to his hut and threw himself into passionate prayer. He was thoroughly disappointed with himself. But it was no use. The damage was done. He could not banish from his mind's eye the tantalizing suppleness of young Jenaguru. He had always encountered her wrapped in the black cloth of a spirit medium and had not thought for a minute that beneath it lay that coppery sweetness. His mind almost could not bear the memory of the moist sensuality of her body. For the hundredth time, desire swept across his body and he groaned aloud as he covered his face in shame. That night, he could not sleep. He dreamt scandalous dreams in which he violated women he had encountered in his past; nuns from a convent in Madeira and uncouth young women who had poured out everything to him in the confessional. He woke up all tense with a drawn face and swollen eyes. He could not eat a morsel.

After a week of futile prayer and meditation, the Jesuit conceded defeat and decided to approach the king and ask for a wife. He had on his arrival scornfully declined a maiden the king had offered him and recouping her was not likely to be a problem. Terrible guilt assailed him as it became clear that his solemn vow of celibacy would now not stand for long. He took a grudging comfort from the knowledge that he was only a man and only God knew what really went on in the holy monasteries and abbeys where the devout abided. Simple Tete, ignorant of any vocation, had gladly accepted the woman offered him by the king and she was already with child. He looked like the happiest man on earth. Yet, the thought of any other woman sickened the priest. It was Jenaguru he wanted, and Christianity could continue taking care of itself as it had always done.

That evening, he called Tete to his hut, swore him to secrecy and, admonishing him to act with absolute discretion, sent him to arrange a meeting with Jenaguru at the pool on the morrow. She declined; telling the messenger that she did not consort with foreigners and the priest should stop trying to convert her to his religion. Fr Silveira suffered pangs of agony and for more than a full month Tete had his work cut out shuttling between the two adversaries with tidings of felicity. The Jesuit was very much shocked by the sweetness with which he coaxed her, but she was adamant. She said he should have taken the wife offered him by her brother, after all, it was an honour to have bride price waived and did his spirits not forbid him to take a woman?

Then, one day, quite out of the blue, she shocked Tete with a simple question: 'Do you think he can make me happy, this man with a skin like pus?'

Well, one thing led to another and Fr Silveira was finally able to meet Jenaguru at the pool. She was of royal beauty and it was clear that she enhanced her looks using secret methods unknown to ordinary folk. Her hair stretched straight from her head like the armor of a fighting porcupine and her skin glowed like the freshly ripe fruit of the buffalo thorn. She exuded a fresh and earthy fragrance suggesting honey and the petals of wild flowers. When she opened her mouth to speak, her black lips seemed to laugh of their own and her perfect white teeth shone like polished ivory. She had obviously prepared for the rendezvous and Fr Silveira felt strangely honoured.

He was exasperated by the necessity of speaking through Tete who stood bemused at his side.

'Stranger,' she said without preamble, 'What are you offering me?'

'I am in love with you,' said Fr Silveira with nervous naivety.

'Don't be foolish,' she said, 'would I be here if that were not settled?'

'Leave us!' he said, somewhat harshly, to Tete.

*

Fr Goncalo da Silveira was a very happy man for several months. Love was sweet and Jenaguru was discreet. His heart was in Africa and Portugal was a foreign land to him. The grand palaces of Europe were nothing compared to the stone fort of Danamombe. He preached and ministered. He traveled far and wide. He baptized in the name of the Holy Spirit, served the Holy Communion to his flock and watered it with benevolence. Contentment and pleasure soon restored to him his good health and his waistline bulged with fat beneath his cassock. Africa, to him, was paradise.

But the fates would not have it. Mapunza Gutu's senior wife, out of sheer misguidedness, one fine morning congratulated His Highness on the conception of the royal heir. Puzzled, the king admonished the woman to quickly explain what she meant. The tale then emerged of how Jenaguru expected to deliver a child within the next three months. Livid with rage, the Munhumutapa ordered a full investigation. A trap was set. The Jesuit was   caught in the act and tried by a court of elders. He was condemned to death.

Munhumutapa Mapunza Gutu, for the love of his sister accepted a secret plea bargain negotiated faithfully by Tete, and banished the lovers with the decree that he must not set his eyes upon them again. It happened at that time that the king's soldiers went to Muti Usina Zita to seek allegiance and the wedded couple made good their escape. They kept off the beaten track and kept all pursuers off their scent. But within a few miles of the coast, they came upon some warlike savages who murdered the whole party in cold blood.

When, in due course the Arab traders of Danamombe reached the coast, they learnt with surprise that the missionary's party had not been seen there. They could only conclude that the Karanga had secretly pursued them and exacted upon them the barbaric execution of driving an iron nail through the head.

That version of the story has survived to this day.

Notes

A royal expedition chartered by the Silveira family to conquer the Mutapa is recorded as having fallen prey to warlike tribes. Some say that they were not accustomed to the terrain, ran out of food and succumbed to tropical diseases. However, Karanga records show that they reached Danamombe in fair numbers and were well received. The true story of their compatriot's sojourn was told them and they could not but believe it. They were shown the explicit diaries of an amorous Fr. Silveira, which had been given to the Mutapa as momentos of a great friendship. They conceded that their mission was accomplished.

Unfortunately, the whole party perished on its way to the coast, devoured alive by a large pack of wild dogs. The King of Portugal in this way never got to answer the one question that his subject, the Munhumutapa, had asked the envoys to put to him: 'How can the hyena partake of the zebra before the lion has eaten?'

He Is Not Dead
by Joop Bersee

He is not dead, yet I can
See the fat turn white, his
Mouth shrinking, loss of
Water and life, eyeballs
Leathery dreaming, dates
Cut off from the stem,
Its river in the ground,
Root mouth closed and
Locked by a muddy bone.

The destroyer invades,
Dog bites, a machine not
Thinking, ripping, tearing,
The snout convinced by
The silk slicing of skin.
The dog snaps and cracks
Deeper, river emptied out,
Pale loss, trying, convincing,
Bone by bone into mud.

TWO POEMS
by Jana Van Niekerk

Little Boy, my baby1

I'm only a little helpless baby
if the wolves must eat me
they must eat me.

I hold on to you a bit
you are also alone

you wake up shouting and farting
I have to hold you while you poo
you're only the second man whose underwear I've sniffed
you can spend an hour alone looking at the wall
I need to be in the same room as you
you are heavy when you sleep
you snuffle like a piggie
I want you to maul me

like old times, except for the small red cut above my

little boy

in my bed full of wee
even a splash of blood
yeasty poo and curdsy breast-milk
fresh-baked semen
the smell on my fingers
marmite
salty marine
my pork lunch

my perfect child.

already you know
crying
the pain of hunger gas wetness a needle
already there is dirt under your fingernails

I thought you
portaled here through me
but look you are the gateway

I smell like a zoo
I love you so much in your sour jersey
I empty this breast into you like a machine-gun

Ass-Man

I am an Ass-Man.

I like asses.

His, not hers.

I like your ass.

the way it follows you to the bathroom.

the way it cooks dinner.

it rises, it wants me to

slip it to you.

I get sad when I watch porn
o
because your ass is better than that,
it is meant for better things

basically

I want your ass
I want your ass
and it wouldn't be so bad
assed
if I got lucky once in a while
it would smile.

Thabo Of Mandelaville
by Tebogo Fokone

Imagine walking through a busy mall during a sidewalk sale on payday.
Now you know how much space we have.
Imagine seeing your sons soiled sports socks, soaking in an overflowing septic tank
Now you know what we smell
Imagine glass streets, plastic plants, paper grass, and tin flowers
Now you know how clean we are
Imagine empty tankers; empty cargo planes; empty freight trains
Now you know how much we have to eat
Imagine dreaming dreams that belong to somebody else
Now you know how closely we sleep
Imagine that what you're imagining is not imagining, but real
Now you know Mandelaville

A Hard Place

by Allan Kolski Horwitz

Saturday night. Karen Brown gets ready to leave home in Hermanus to pick up her two teenage daughters from a party in Gordon's Bay. She has agreed to do the fetching because her husband, Pete, who had dropped the girls off in the late afternoon, had soon afterwards twisted his ankle during a run on the beach. Early in the coming week it will be Madiba's 93rd birthday and the local school has encouraged all children to celebrate the historic occasion. Luckily another parent had volunteered to do the honours, so most of the class have gone to Bettina Opperman's. Karen smiles recalling how Jodi and Antoinette had looked before going off: tight tank tops and jeans, their young faces bright with excitement, brace-filled mouths shiny with lip gloss. Reaching for the car keys, Karen kisses Pete goodbye and pats the dogs. She is a good mother and despite the late hour and her fatigue, she will gladly endure the forty-five minute drive there and the forty-five minute drive back.

Andile hobbles over to the outside toilet. The door doesn't close properly and the smell from the pit is foul. But it has always been that way so he doesn't curse and quickly lowers himself onto the broken plank of a seat. He shits and feels some relief. The meat they had eaten yesterday at Bossie's was maybe a bit off; anyway at least it was something. He wipes himself with newspaper then shuffles back to the shack. Zandra is there with their two sons. The boys are asleep but she is listening to the radio. The music is kak but there is nothing else to do – the tv was bust - so he can't tell her to switch it off; at best, he can just tell her to try another station.

Karen pulls into the Opperman's driveway. Anna and Andre are lovely people. Anna is on the school committee and active in the church. Karen admires her poise and friendliness but is also a little intimidated by her ability to organize and get things done. Their eldest daughter, Bettina, is Jodi's best friend, so the Brown's have quite a bit of contact with them. It was Anna's idea to give the kids a party. After all, didn't Madiba save the whole country – not just the Blacks? And the girls were overjoyed to fulfill the principal's recommendation. Imagine being 93 years old and still clear-headed. If it was a miracle to have survived 27 years in jail, then to reach such a ripe old age was another - especially given the stress of having been president of a troublesome country! When Karen enters the house, she finds a number of other parents in the living room. All are White except for Cynthia Mashaba. Cynthia is a magistrate in Somerset West and speaks English fluently. Her daughter, Thembi, is currently top of the grade and a real achiever. Karen accepts a glass of wine but only a small one – the drive home, with its zigzagging mountain bends, demands concentration, and every now and again on the weekends the police have roadblocks to check for drunken driving.

Andile sprawls on the bed which takes up much of the shack. The three boys are curled on a mattress pushed against one of the corners. Zandra is dozing now, her legs under the blanket. Andile switches off the radio. The silence is not really silence: there is still the sound of Piet's television next door and Ous Anna's drunken laughter two shacks away. There is also Zandra's occasional snore. Andile switches off the paraffin lamp. His stomach is still sore despite the shit. He will have to wait till morning and hope that the clinic has something good for that. Last week, like most times, they were out of everything except panado. But the nurse is a good woman. She tries her best with the little medicine she has. Come to think of it, his stomach has been sore for more than six months now. Funny how it started when he lost his job at the packing station.

The girls are jammed in the car. In addition to Jodi and Antoinette, there's Cassandra and Anna-Marie – both live in the same part of Hermanus in one of the new townhouse complexes. The party had been a lot of fun but the boys who were supposed to come hadn't made it, so it had been an all-girl affair which was fine but not perfect. Of course, moms and dads said there was plenty of time for boys, after all, they were only fourteen, but still it would have more fun if the boys had come. Three months ago, when Cassandra had had a birthday party, there had been as many boys as girls. Ja, that had been an awesome party - with a dj and proper dance floor and streamers and snacks and everything. Now they were on the way up the pass and everyone was still pretty wide awake from the games.

Andile can't sleep. One of the boys turns in his sleep, a dog barks outside. He switches the radio on again. There is a program about Madiba's birthday. The announcer talks about the Old Man's wonderful sense of caring. He says he is in Qunu celebrating with his family. Some White millionaires have donated money to build a big school there. As the announcer says that Madiba wants everything possible to be done to help the youth get a good life, Andile hears a knock at the door. It's probably Solomon. But he's early. They weren't supposed to go out before one o'clock. Andile swears. They have hardly eaten today and everyone is hungry. So to do the job is worth it. Of course, there is a choice, but most times, like tonight, it doesn't feel like there's a choice. It's lucky Solomon is a strong somebody who knows what to do. They had worked together at the packing station. Both had been forklift drivers. Then, once the retrenchment money was eaten, it was Solomon who found a way to bring in some bucks. Andile can't complain – they share everything even though he is a beginner and still a bit slow, a bit squeamish.

Karen revs the car up the hill. She wants to get home as quickly as possible now. The whiskey she drank after the wine, had at first given her a kick, but the effect quickly wore off and made her even more tired. Damn, why did her body always let her down with alcohol! Most of their friends could drink her under the table – not that they were such heavy drinkers, except for the Malans', of course, who both hit the bottle too often and became quite rowdy at dinner parties. Anyway, the kids had enjoyed the evening and the DVD Anna played about Mandela's life had been very educational.

"Woza, you lazy dog!" Solomon is saying, half serious, half joking. "I don't want to get there too late. After one o'clock there's not many cars." Andile struggles to a sitting position, and puts on his shoes. "Sien jou later", Zandra says, as she closes her eyes and goes back to sleep. Sometimes a woman has to keep quiet. As long as he brings back some money, and sometimes food and clothes, from these night trips, what does it matter where they come from. The kids are growing and life is hell without a man working. On her side, cleaning houses is all she can do but there are too many foreigners around who will work for nothing. Eyes half-closed, she watches Andile rise to his feet, then steady himself. Shit, he looks pale despite his dark complexion. The man is truly sick. But you have to give it to him – when it comes to standing up for the family, he's prepared to walk that extra mile. And that is something, compared to all the other men around – including the good-for-nothing father of her first born.

The pass is dark. There is a moon but it is obscured by the hill they are climbing. The car, a second hand one Pete had picked up in Cape Town, is taking strain with its full load. Karen is a good driver and knows when to change down gears. The girls are singing a song – some pop tune that has dominated facebook and their little heads for a few weeks now. Karen feels her cheeks flush. She shakes her long hair free. Amazing how her own youth seemed so far away! Now she is a mother to two beautiful girls and has wrapped them in the cocoon of home, school and church. What good fortune to be living in a time of reconciliation and justice! Not that she follows politics too much – the endless scandals and power plays – but she has a good feeling about this new South Africa. The workers at the packing plant are obliging and productive. Her role in human resources is to supervise training courses and Black advancement. Pity they had to retrench so many people last year. But Head Office was under pressure to deliver higher returns to shareholders. It was also a pity because the casuals they have used since then are not half as skilled and complaints from supermarkets about poor quality fruit are rising.

Andile and Solomon make their way through the squatter camp. The shacks are pressed close together and the alleyways between them switch direction abruptly. Moving quietly, they leave the last one and reach the highway. The moon is still high but there is a point at the turn of a bend where it won't matter if its light shines brightly. Cars usually come round at a high enough speed to be completely surprised by the rocks they find spread across the Gordon's Bay side of the road. Usually there is no time to react. In any case, if by a miracle a driver is able to apply the brakes, the car simply swerves off the road instead of just smashing into the rocks, bursting a tire, and veering to a stop.

Karen expertly glides up the hill and beetles along the straight section of highway that passes the reservoir. The pine forests stretch on either side. Though summer fires have thinned them, the smell of resin still touches the air and the half moon lights the way. The girls have grown quiet; they seem to be sleeping, heads on shoulders, as Karen switches on the radio to keep awake. "Our beloved Madiba is turning 93 on Tuesday. Just imagine the life he can look back on, the good he has done, the chances taken to free all South Africans!" The announcer then dedicates a song to the 'Father of the Nation' and invites listeners to contribute Mandela stories and to nominate songs in his honour. "Remember, on Tuesday, dedicate 67 minutes of your time to doing a good deed as inspired by Madiba. What better present for him than to offer a good deed in his name!" Karen nods her head in agreement. Yes, though so much has changed, there are still many problems. For everyone to take just an hour off their ordinary selfish lives and do good for another person is surely a noble thing. She yawns. The kids have all Sunday morning to recover but she will have to get up early to feed the dogs and let in the gardener.

Arriving at the sharpest point of the bend, Andile and Solomon haul out the rocks they had used four days previously. Far off they can hear a car. It is not a very powerful one but it is still rolling along at quite a pace. "Come, let us put them out quickly," Solomon urges. Around one o'clock, traffic dies down and it would be stupid to miss this opportunity. As Andile bends to roll the first boulder into place, he suddenly catches himself singing, and a grin covers his face. Yes, this is the right song to be singing. Even though the presents will not be for Madiba.

Karen takes the first bend after the straight allowing the steering wheel to lock perfectly into the curve. She enjoys this aspect of driving, this proving that a woman can also handle a machine. She comes out of the bend into another straight and accelerates.

The rocks are neatly spaced across the highway; two particularly big ones in the centre and four smaller ones on either side so that even if a driver manages to avoid the centre ones, the car will collide with the side ones and be forced to stop.

The radio announcer says: "Folks, it's been a pleasure. I hope you all take the occasion to heart and deliver on your promise to do good deeds. Imagine, just 67 minutes of your day and bring light into the world! It's now time for the 1am news read by . . ."

The car takes the bend just as Andile, kierie in hand, hidden behind a bush parallel to the line of rocks, sings ". . . Happy birthday to you, happy birthday . . ."

Woman Of All Times
by Nolizo Chiya

Woman have blood wisdom of mother nature
in their premenstrual distress, walking the celestial
barefooted with burning estrogen
flowing blood of menstruation and the upheaval of menopause

listen to the rhythm of their thighs that shield profanity
different from her sisters yet equally special using love to confiscate
old burning wounds they bear mystery from the passage of their veins
fluids of their flesh celebrating vaginas and stirring life

in their bodies floating waters of childbirth spurting of kind milk
they know in their bones the cipher of feminine secrecy
the great unknown consuming death
the beasts run from their grandmothers

frequently flawed for being the opposition
they are attuned to rebirth after weeks of hibernation

TWO POEMS
by Mphutlane Wa Bofelo

This poem would not have a title though it could

The present is
In the eye of the beholder
History in the fancy
Of the interpreter
The fate of the past
At the feet of the narrator
Or is it in the whims of the writer

The future is a speck
Of dust on the coat
Of a dreamer
Today is tomorrow's yesterday

Yesterday is a heritage or an antique
Buildings are ruins or monuments
Depending on the eye-sight
Or is it the insight of the viewer

Today is an illusion or a reality
Art is life or commodity
Foreigners are aliens
or tourists\ immigrants
Fish is food or game
Hunting is livelihood or a sport
Rivers are rivers or exotic sites
Mountains are mountains or scenic spots
According to the lenses of the camera
Some say it is not so much
The vision but the position
Of the photographer
Tomorrow is a cliché or a certainty
Incidents are experiences or statistics
Culture is civilization or superstitions
Subject to the affinities of the observer
Or the objective of the observation
Do we ever subject ourselves to the view of the subject?

Lolita

It was a secret open
To the whole hood
Your old man had
The habit of fondling
Little girls when
He had one too many
Everybody whispered
Questions about
How your sisters'
Babies were fathered
When no boy could
Dare to touch them
In view of the poisonous
Stick of your dad
& the religious manner
They kept away from men

I just shook my head
Every time my friends asked
Why the little girl next door
Wore the face of a woman
Though I also noticed
Something matured in your smile
Every time you talked dirty
& my body told me things
Anytime I watched you walk
I peeped through
The window and saw
You sandwiched
Between my big brother
And his cousin
You were only twelve
At sixteen I was still
Confused about the messages
The scene sent to my body
Years later I found myself
Humming a ballad
Between your thighs
The night before
I had seen you
Jump out of the jalopy
Of the archbishop
I am yet to find a melody
Equivalent to the seasoned harmony
Of the music of our bodies that day
I think I have an idea

What crazy idea
Raced through the mind
Of the city mayor
When he decided to divorce
His wife of forty-years
To make you
The mother of his children
When you are half
The age of his lastborn

in all (fair)ness

by Jennifer Rees

tags: africa; lady justice; poetry; decay; resilience
lady justice is blind(folded)
on the streets of cape town

where fumy paint adorns
freshly acknowledged shells
trending on twitter
loving the glitter
(until the next big thing)

but lady justice is
waiting
for more rape
more village-pillage
of already-ruins

or to age gracefully
on slow-to-die walls

to be loved in lenses
and/or
words

to say:
here lies lady justice
amongst wire
stones and
city-shit

to be looked upon
(like danté retching out words)

on his blindness
in her blindness
in all (fair)ness

*(struck by this lady-on-a-wall in the heart of cape town and decided to get lost so we'd have
to drive down the same road again.)*

Reflections On My Rejected Novel

by Darcy du Toit

Last Friday I came across my Novel again, and quite a strange feeling it was. I'd almost forgotten about it – more than nine years had passed since it got rejected for the second time and I washed my hands of it, with some relief. True, I'd never deleted it from my computer; maybe that would have been too irrevocable. But I certainly didn't want to be reminded of it. I was a Failed Novelist, my ego had been bruised, I'd put it all behind me. But that day I happened to be searching for something on my computer when it popped up, and I saw that familiar name, and without thinking clicked on it and started reading.... Needless to say, I was appalled. Yes, parts were well written, sometimes very well written, gripping me all over again, even bringing tears to my eyes. But most of it sagged, at times really badly. There was no getting away from it – page after page of banal detail (which I'd fondly imagined was painting a rich background), clumsy dialogue to bridge gaps which I couldn't bear leaving to the reader's imagination, avoiding swear words and descriptions of sexual intimacy even where it was called for – but I've said enough. The words of the publisher's reader ('verbose', 'turgid', 'self-indulgent', 'contrived') which I'd found so unbelievably crass and hurtful now struck me as an understatement. Well done, publisher's reader! Though I'd raged at your lack of sensitivity, and darkly suspected that my race and gender had something to do with it, you were spot on.

But there was something else you said, which I found unbearably patronising at the time, which now caught my interest: 'somewhere underneath the dross there's a story waiting to be told'. Maybe, I thought, that just about sums it up. The dross, well, no argument about that. But there certainly was a story and – it was then that it struck me – maybe, after all this time, I might finally be able to tell it. Maybe I'd been too close to it the first time, too overwhelmed, too brim-full of politically correct principles that I wanted to find pegs for, that I lost sight of what really needed to be said. Maybe I'm detached enough now to do a better job.

Then all my doubts came back: how can I get involved in it again without getting lost in the same emotional labyrinth and ending up with a slightly more mature version of the same monstrosity? The next morning – Saturday – I woke up with the answer: 'disaggregate'. I'd seen the word in a headline on the financial pages of the Cape Times, and had only a vague idea what it meant, but it had stuck in my memory and now, suddenly, it expressed exactly what I had to do. The structure I'd contrived had been far too convoluted – no wonder I'd resorted to all sorts of devices to string it all together. But, in reality, it wasn't a single story or, if it was, it would have needed a Tolstoy to tell it. In fact, it was a series of narratives – stories of individuals who had nothing to do with each other, whose lives had intersected in odd ways, sometimes briefly, sometimes moving in tandem for a while before branching off and intersecting with the lives of others, but each time changing the course of events, changing those lives inexorably, and twice resulting in tragedy.

That's really what it was about. Those two tragedies, separated by thirty years of the new South Africa's birth pains and yet so intimately bound together that they were really one - that was the 'story' I was trying to tell. That, dear anonymous publisher's reader, was what you were trying to tell me. But do so, being no Tolstoy, I must simply tell the stories of the different dramatis personae and let them do the rest.

By now you may have guessed: it's not really a novel. It is (as they say in the movies) 'based on a true story'. And yes, I'm one of the dramatis personae; but my part is only a minor one (even though, like all the others, it was vital for a moment). So it isn't about me – no, it really isn't. I was only a spectator most of the time, seeing bits of the drama through the eyes of others, a conduit-pipe at most, creating links between people that would otherwise not have existed, passing on information without knowing what I was doing and without the slightest idea of the consequences it could have. I could write about how I experienced it all, I suppose, but it would be pure self-indulgence, distracting attention from the story I want to tell. So I made an early resolution: I would write about myself in the third person, just like everyone else, and be as objective about my own actions as possible, giving myself no greater a role than I deserve as just one of the characters unwittingly preparing a tragedy – not out of feigned modesty, I repeat, but simply because it isn't about me. And for the rest I would preserve the novelist's supposed independence –free to range through space and time, no longer bound by the chronology of what happened or the built-in limitations of the characters I felt duty-bound to describe as they were, no more, no less. I would transcend photographic representation and let myself go into the realms of abstractions, free to describe the essence of what happened, as I understand it.

As this might indicate, telling it as a novel is important for another reason also: I don't know all the facts. No-one does, no-one can; those who knew the most are dead or will never speak, and a supposedly real-life account filled with gaps and conjecture will lack all credibility. So turning it into a novel is the only way of telling it. It also has the advantage of allowing me to change names and places and avoid treading on toes, to describe what I know, imagine what I don't know and decide on the meaning of it all. Which is what? Perhaps it's the inevitability of those tragedies, rooted so deeply in the drama of the times; or perhaps it's the excruciating coincidence of it all – as in a Priestley time play, it could all have been avoided had something happened slightly differently (had I not done what I did, so naturally, so helpfully). Or could it? It happened. Maybe that's all that matters.

At moments like this I realise my limitations as a writer. What I'm trying to capture are two different sides of the drama: the inexorable way it gathered momentum out of diverse, unrelated origins; but, equally, the totally accidental nature of those origins as well as the sheer randomness of incidents which caused events to move, sometimes catastrophically, in one direction rather than another.

But let me learn from my mistakes. Let me stop waffling about what I'm trying to say. Let me just say it.

Ingrid Jonker
by Abigail George

She is a ghost of her former self, but she is still in the land of the living — a tragic beauty in a state of turmoil and crisis. "There is no time like the future to seal my fate," she thinks to herself. She is unbearably nervous tonight and smokes cigarette after cigarette, dashes them in an ashtray. She paces up and down, but she still attaches no serious damage or blame to her last love affair. She was gentle and loving with Simone today. In Paris, she was already a writer in exile — cursed, perturbed and a voyeur who had high-maintenance taste. She is still unclear about what she is going to do.

Her resolve unraveled that night in the flat. Her beauty meant nothing to her. She was not conceited. What had it brought her but ill-fated relationships, rejection, pain and suffering? Nothing dulled or sated her desire for love, for life, for a hot and heavy intellectual debate, which her voice was the center of. In retrospect, living in a state of Apartheid had made her begin to doubt what she was living for. She wanted to be taken seriously as a woman, but more importantly, as a writer. The writers and poets of that time were in conflict with a patriarchal system. The essence of identity being passed to her was a fate worse than death and could not guarantee security in a career.

Love will change you in an indescribable way. It will make strong hearts weak, render the intellectual speechless, comedians will vanish and be replaced by philosophers; everything that was laughable before becomes serious and stimulating. Death is the ultimate sacrifice, invisible and mysterious. Ingrid Jonker made a decision for herself that was useless. There is no earthly justification for what she did — removing the very substance of her gift, her genius from this world, by taking her own life, by drowning herself in the sea.

As they pulled the limp body from the ocean, the subject in death mirrored life. There was a chill in her embrace. Her fingers were numb. She was haunting, pale and beautiful, lacking tenderness. Her cheeks were wet as if from tears. Her mouth was full. Her lips were cool, as if she had drunk her fill. Her appetite was sated. She slept as if to dream. She did not speak and there was no lapsed recovery from the multiple meanings of words. There would no longer be the willing prerogative of an insomniac to stay up the whole night and blot out the stain of her sins by writing.

The male policemen's hair was windswept. They talked amongst themselves. The breeze was salty, the morning tide came in, the breakers crashed against the rocks, the foam raced towards the shore, birds circling overhead perched on rocks and altered states were trapped in a war of nerves.

Her eyes stared into the pale, blue sky. The beginning of the day was like her work - imaginative. It gave recognition to curious incidents in the still, mournful air of the morning. It concerned itself with the decline of evil and the harmful beginnings of the harvest of desolation. The shadow of a haunting memory refused to disappear into a hazy reverie. The poet, Ingrid Jonker, was dead. Her face had an unsmiling seriousness on it. Even in death she was angelic. Her demeanor never giving way to the trouble or unfounded insecurity that lay underneath. She was authentic, a true original. But she never knew this in her lifetime although she knew what the imagination is capable of, the loneliness of the heart and when it is ready to surrender to a temporary escape into a romance.

Her innocence and vulnerability remind me of women ahead of the times they were born into, women who were visionaries, leaders, and had to endure great humiliation from powerful men based in the public realm. Women like Joan of Arc, Saartjie Baartman,

Susan Sontag, Princess Diana, Sylvia Plath and Marilyn Monroe.

She is barefoot in her flat. Her hair is dark, wild and free and falls across her face. Yet in her eyes there is a declaration of having been to hell and back again. There has been a radical change in her behavior since she came back from Paris. This hasn't escaped her. But she doesn't speak of her experiences there, of the lingering sadness that torments her. The 'unhappiness' does not have a name yet, but soon the world will know and there is nothing she can do to protect her daughter from it. Fate is like a drowned thing, an empty shell reserved for the sound of silence invoking the sound of the ocean. She has decided she is a poor activist, wife, mother, woman and lover. Simone, her daughter, wants to make her smile but she is tired of playing games. Nonetheless she plays along, pretends to catch the joke, and today, when the journalist came for the interview, there was a glimmer of a smile on her face when her picture was taken. The picture of her as the famous, prize-winning poet — the female voice of her generation — was a small consolation to her. Without her father's love she felt lost. Fame meant little or nothing and the turning point came now, this night. How different would things be in the morning for people from whom she had been estranged for years?

How many times, I wonder, did she have to redirect her focus when tears blurred her vision - when she cried, when she was working? How do you survive a blessed and cursed childhood? What made her laugh, this sensitive, delicate woman? Who made her smile? The elementary particles of light became diffused on her face. It was translucent, her face was dreamy and her lashes were damp. There is a distracting air near the incident now as they wait for the coroner. Simone woke up in the stillness of the flat and went in search of her mother. She searched the rooms one by one and found they were empty.

Where does this story begin? The car is hurtling down the road past everything a young Ingrid knows and loves. This is the world of a child, a babyish language, tea parties in the shade with her sister, barefoot on the sandy beach searching for beautiful feathers, smooth pebbles and colorful shells. Now history has turned the page. Their father has come to fetch them to live with him and his family. Their idyllic childhood is over. As the car moves forward, the shiny wheels turning around and around without an end in sight like this trip — a car ride — they are being dragged to a new future, further and further away from their old haunts. As they turn the corner they will be a stone's throw from where they watched the fishing boats at sea. Ingrid glances across at her sister on the backseat. Her eyes are bright, but she does not look out at the world. Ingrid's shoulders are hunched over as she stares out of the window and looks at the sea of her childhood. She doesn't know it yet, but she will never see it again. Yet she knows with a certainty it will always be there. Other people will fall in love with it like she has, easily. Her father is very serious but he doesn't scare her. Ingrid doesn't scare easily.

She has already fallen in love with his spectacles, his shoes and the black suit he is wearing. He took his hat off in her grandmother's house. Ingrid wanted to take it from him and hold it in her hands. She had never seen anything quite like it before. He does not say a word to her. He ignores Ingrid and her sister completely. He looks like a bear. Ingrid would like him to pick her up and hold her. She wants him to take her hand in his and say in his gruff manner, "What are the names of your dolls? What do you like to read? Do you miss your mother?" But he says nothing and bundles them into the car. In her head Ingrid has an imaginary conversation with her father. He is silent. He stares ahead into the blue distance.

"Why didn't you come to see us before? Why did you wait so long? There were so many things I wanted to show you. Sometimes when we have tea parties we set a place for you. I don't know how you like your tea, with milk or without, with sugar or without, with lemon or without. I had a birthday this year. I'm a year older. I missed you, daddy. Daddy, are you listening? I love you. I always loved you. I thought you just forgot about me, about Anna, but one day I believed you'd come back to fetch us and we'd be a family again. But the important thing is that you're here now. My wish came true."

Mr. Jonker begins to perspire. He takes out a beautifully starched handkerchief and wipes his brow. He is a man of few words. Ingrid wonders how the world looks through spectacles. She leans back into the leather seat. His cheeks are puffy like he is chewing sticky sweets. Ingrid is very still. Her sister's eyes are no longer bright but watery. Her life as she knows it is disappearing before her eyes. She kicks her foot against the seat as she straightens up. Her eyes are fixed on the beach, the mouths of the dunes, the quivering branches of trees in the wind.

Her sister starts crying on the backseat of the car. Ingrid hugs her and begins to stroke her hair, saying comforting things in her ear, whispering to her so she will not disturb her father. Now she is close to tears herself. She does not know this stranger, the even stranger place where they were going. She wonders how she will cope. Will he permit her to write her stories and poetry and let the sisters have their barefoot tea parties in the garden? Or will they be outsiders? Mr. Jonker is not a man moved easily by tears. Ingrid cannot translate what she is feeling into words yet. She is lost in space. This is where it began, Ingrid Jonker said to herself in a flat in Sea Point thirty-two years later. This state of affairs was an accident waiting to happen.

Through shame, spite, the government's own brand of vitriolic censorship, the father and daughter remained estranged for decades. Did she know they had the same personality, the same aggressive style of debate? That they stuck to their principles and would not let go? She was her father's daughter. How could he reject her, how could she undermine him? They were both writers. Could they not see how alike they were? How could this escape both of them?

She realized as a child that it is very hard to fall in love with something and give yourself to it completely. She communed with nature as a child because it was there that she felt most comfortable, most wild and most free. In her poetry she wrote about the harvest of desolation, the anguish of trials by fire and error, past mistakes, lives that were wrecked by emotional scarring, the youth who were detached from and attached to violence, marches, protests, Bantu education, boycotts and the eeriness of loneliness and mental illness.

She is standing barefoot on the sandy beach. The sunlight plays on the water but she is shivering, trembling. The sky's blue dissolve lingers overhead. Ingrid Jonker is meeting her father for the first time today. She wonders if she looks anything like him. She wonders if he'll like her stories and her poems and what he will think of the idea of her being a writer one day when she is grown up.

His approval is already important to her. She cannot wait for his arrival, to welcome him. She does not know yet that she and her sister will cry themselves to sleep in their father's new home. She does not know yet that life is the cause and effect of accidents waiting to happen. She needs his love, his guidance, but she is unprepared for the future that awaits her in her stepmother's new home. Everything was already wrecked before she turned around and ran back to the house as she scrambled to put her shoes on. She didn't waste any time with regret as an adult, but she finally found the words to translate the hunger and pain that had consumed her as a child, careening away from the only home she had known. It was the same heartache; the same human stain that the mothers and daughters, wives and sisters of the lost but cherished and beloved men of this country had during the legacy of Apartheid.

Fields of Summer
by Yoshira

an outcast
a prickly cactus
standing
amongst smiling blossoms
soft tiny whispers
false hurtful rumors
foolish assumptions
test the stamina of my self worth
but
betrayed
by yellow sunrays
turned into a deadly killer – scorching heat
delicate blossom petals
wither
thirsty stems
begging
for a drop of heavens tears
I smile
my thorns that once were mocked
ensure survival
my velvet green skin shines

I am
unmoved

TWO POEMS
by Jana Van Niekerk

My little locker

Truly tattered
my little locker
sien jou om die draai
it's nice to get a little pished and see what happens

all i can say is my feelings are my feelings

quite a ride

this glorious existence
don't feel pressured

(I know)

I make a lumpy white sauce
and wonder how this music got on my System

I must be made for greater things

I tidy up after myself
It's always just what I needed

I've got it going on,
by the grace of god,
afraid to say God,

paradise came to me like this poem did,
in daywear

A poem for myself

I woke up and wrote a poem
one bit was started in the night
snakes are my sign
slowing
Dream
when all else fails

what would a poem say about me
it would say everything
I cannot
it would promise me
it would arrive.

the poem says
I am not here
you would see me by its shape
it takes me not from me,

I listen and it speaks.

Self-Conscious
by Yoric Watterott

I watch him
I notice how he leans into the wall,
Sinking into the background
With one leg jittering,
Hammering morse-code into the ground
I watch how his lips purse over the rim,
Funneling down yet another cup of coffee
The caffeine anxiously fidgets through his veins,
Eyes darting around the bistro, constantly aware of me
I watch him
Using me to investigate himself,
Observing every defect
No one sees me but you…
Our little secret…

Inja

by Mpiyane

Inja yam nguSipoti,
Ihlala njalo ihluthi.
Ndiyithanda kakhulu,
Iyandinyamekela kakhulu.
Indilumkisa ngokukhonkotha,
Igxoth' amasela angabi nakuzithathela.
Ndiyiphethe kakuhle njengosana,
Andinakuyilibala naxa igula.
Kushushu kubanda ise yinja yam,
Kunetha kunomoya yona ikwa yeyam.
Namhlanje nangomso akuyi kutshintsha nto,
Yona likhaya lalo eli lihle alishoti nganto.
Masibe nombulelo ngezilwanyana,
Zadalelwa injongo yokuba sizinyamekele.
Owu intle madoda yeyam ndiyayibanga,
Akwaba nani beninokuba nezenu
Ngumhlobo wendoda nebhinqa,
Masincede singabi nako ukuyibulala,
Yiyo yona iya thandeka,
Thand' inja yakho njengam.

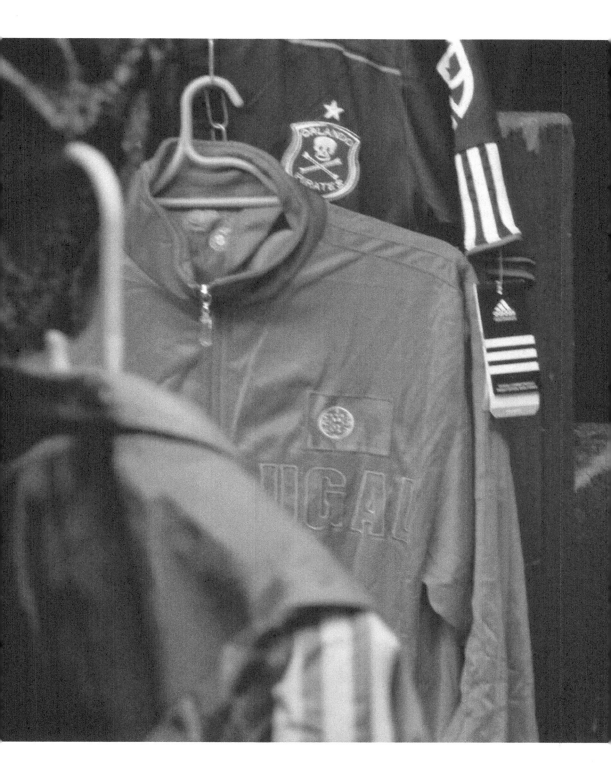

TWO POEMS
by Nomkhubulwane

Bayede maqhawekazi bayede!

Qhawekaz'uyesabeka
Isibindi sakh'esebhubesi
Ubuhle bakho buyancomeka
Hawu qhawekaz'uyidayimane kithi
Ngimatasatasa yingubo yemfudumalo
Ingub'owangembesa yona
Ngingumfanekiso wakho kwezokulingisa
Uyingcweti mama, ndlovukazi, qhawekazi
Ngijabula ngijule njengendlovukaz'uDudu Khoza wo Khozi
Mama siyabonga ngothando lwakho
Ngiziqhenye kungqangqazele'umhlaba
Ngijabulele leso sibeletho semfudumalo
Bayede kuwe mkhathi intombifikile
Bayede nakuy'indlovukaz'uNomkhubulwane
Owavakashela amaphuph'ami
Ngikhothame nakuy'umntwana uMagogo
Owayengungcweti kwezomculo
Lingihayele ngivukwe abadal'iphimbo lesangoma
Isangoma somculo, bayede! Busi Mhlongo
Ungumanqoba wanqob'umdlavuza
Vuleka maphiko ngindize njengokhozi
Ngiyocambalala kuw'amadwala
Ngibuk'amagquma nezintaba zakithi Kwa-Zulu
Ngokucophelela njenge ndlovukazi uMkabayi ka Jama
Ngijule ngibenothando ngifane nendlovukazi u Nandi
Ngibe nobuhlakani bendlovukazi uNomagugu Ngobese
Bayede Fikile bayede! Bayede kunina makhosikazi bayede.

Behind the smile

She smiles to cover her misery
Shielding her scars with heavy layers of make-up
Her voice is in darkness, she's afraid to speak out
The power she has in parliament is not the same as in her home
Mosadi o once's been a queen, now she's just a servant in her home.

Let me tell u what is behind her smile
Her heart is torn apart in pieces, that is true
Her strength and her power is in the boardroom not the bedroom
Have you seen how she speaks in meeting and gatherings uyiqhawekazi?
She drives the masses into insanity as they dance to her toyi-toyi tunes uyigerila
Behind all that her husband sleeps out for days without a word and her child uyitsotsi

Her colleague said to her - leave him alone, get out now
Her friend, a 50-50% kind of woman, said, u have your own money
The house is too big even children abamazi lo bambele umam'isikhundla
Akabuzang'elangeni who is a mistress who feels her shoes makangekho Bo!
Her sister said, angazi uyifunani le nonsense yendoda he is not worth it, leave him
Not knowing when she packs and goes for her meeting
In Britain, Spain zikhiphani lana
Woza la and tell how she finds out who sleeps in her bed

As she drove in her big BMW from the airport
She saw two cars with familiar number plates in a motel near her house.
With anger she stopped - guess who that was in his arms
50-50% best friend who said myeke
With shock she ran to her home driving njengo hlanya
Tears rolling down disappointed
Yes, her husband cheats
That's why she's no longer a queen umtholile today sure

She never asks her sister to come stay with children bakhulile.
She was happy to find her sister endlini as she needed a shoulder to cry on
While all the time she travels her sister warms the bed for her nendoda yakhe akazi
Her kid's abazi they are happy if mancane is home dad akabi strict ngesikhathi ulunge
They only thought it's her magic food that makes ubaba to be home almost the time
The time that akasihlali even when ma is round noma aphekeni mamncane uyiskhokho

She cried and told her tale from the airport trip mamncane was angry more than her
She said, I told you to leave him, he's not worth it mtakama
She's hurt, she even told umama osebenza layikhaya who said, usisi wakho uzithwele
She was so happy not knowing ingane yendoda yakhe, she asked her to stay
Things started shaping waxolel'indoda gave him a third chance kanti akazi
Akaz'umkhuba won'ulayikhaya she never told ingan'ekabani

She was very secretive ngathi she's 20 years kanti she's 30-uphethw'ukusa nje
Mamncane's twins look like her kids nendoda yakhe she's shocked akakwazi nokudla
What is wrong with me, she asked herself?
What have I done to deserve this kind of treatment?
Was it my fault or ngimbi kakhulu beating herself up?
She should have not given him all the chances she did wayengeke ashintshe
She has been brutalized emotionally and spiritually, he's not worth it
She needs to take a break and plan her life without this monster kunzima kakhulu

She's stronger than the three of them put together
Her pride has been destroyed but not her spirit, she will rise again
She will rise with multiple strength though no one stands besides her
Mamncane has lost her pillar and her friend, will never have what they had again
Indoda yakhe has lost a lover, wife, a friend and umama of his wonderful kids
Behind her smile there are wounds and scars but nothing is worth her smile today.

Ba tlang
by Lehlohonolo Shale

Ba tlamehile hoba lebelo
Hoba nako ha se ea bona

Ba tlamehile ho ipatlisisa
Ba be ba iphumane
Ba tlamehile ho toba
Mariha

Tat'omkhulu- My Great Grandfather
by Lwazi Mvusi

Although we have been formerly introduced, we no longer know each other. You were a revered man treading through the deep waters of your final days. I was a reckless infant splashing about in the shallow end with no clue of how to swim through life the way you had. It would seem that regardless of the waves and currents that pulled at you, you were an effortless swimmer. They say each stroke you made was more elegant than the one before. That may just be them idolising you. One must never speak ill of the honourable and the dead. But I'm inclined to agree with them- call it genetic bias.

We buried another one of your children. MaHlati has left us. Now only the youngest two remain. Gogo Ousie's health has been teetering on the edge of the cliff that has been old age. Many times she leaned so far forward that we believed she would fall into the dark abyss below her. Somehow she is able to pull herself back every time. I don't know how much willpower she has left. She looks solid. She is a fighter who pushed on decades after her husband passed away. Despite this, I see the weariness in her eyes. I wonder if she is holding on for the rest of us. She still smiles. Her eyes brighten when her grandchildren walk into a room. The hugs last a little longer. Maybe we still have a few more Christmases with her. I have to remember to make her feel special. But then again, I am six hundred kilometres away from her now.

Your youngest has returned from America. Mkhulu Xhaki is as tall and stately as you. His New Yorker accent captivated our young minds. The years in exile have taken so much from him. I don't know if he has become a different man. Has he become stronger because of it? He bought a house in iXopo but I think he just did that to be closer to you. Closer to Mzimkhulu- the place we all call our home. He is caught between two worlds. The life that he has lived far away from everyone and everything that was familiar to him and the life he could have lived- a life that had you. He is still paying for his sacrifices. You know more about that than I do.

Every time we bury one of your children, we return to Mzimkhulu. It's quite a spectacle. There is always either rain or a strong gust of wind - a marker that a child of the Mvusi clan has passed. A stalwart has been lost. A long convoy of cars with number plates from every part of the country braves the dirt roads and potholes that lead to the house that you and MaNxasana raised your family in. We change from designer heels to flat shoes and sneakers and trek down the hill to the family graveyard. After the burial, we visit the other graves. We come to yours and MaNxasana's; we places stones in remembrance of your children; we lament the loss of your grandchildren who were taken before their time.

I have never lived in Mzimkhulu. None of your great grandchildren ever have. Our parents walk around the house and recount stories of their school holidays spent there with you- their beloved grandfather. They remember the songs they sang in church during the services you delivered. They remember playing in the dusty streets and how stern yet loving you and MaNxasana were. I am mesmerised by how they are transported to another time inside those walls; a time before my existence; a time when they were just children; a moment when none of the cares that have aged them existed. They were just silly, giggly, mischievous, little beings.

You and MaNxasana instilled in them the importance of spending time together as a family. There is a bond between them that makes them look at each other as siblings instead of cousins. They're doing the same with us. They encourage us to spend our vacations and Christmases together. It's worked so far. Hopefully it will have the same far reaching influence as the seed you planted so many years ago. Let's see how long the good times will last for.

I am consumed by a sense of home as I sit outside your house. I take in the open air, the rolling green hills and the strange serenity surrounding me. It is so different to the world of skyscrapers and endless hooting that I come from. I wonder what this scene must have looked like when you sat out here. Are there any differences? Are they extreme differences? Or would you still recognise this land that was once your piece of heaven. Would you still have the same pride in it? Would you be proud of what your family has become?

This nation has changed so much from the one you knew. You were a pioneer of Methodism in black communities. You preached the good word. You believed in it. In the darkest of days and in the moments of such hatred and pain, you still believed. You opened your heart to the possibility of happiness and peace. I hope I am like you in that way. Even though those heart wrenching days are behind us, there is still such a mountain before us to climb. We are climbing it. Your grandchildren, our last link to you, are business people and scientists and teachers. They remember your lessons of education and Godliness and valuing family above all else. Your great grandchildren are dreamers. We see the world in a different way. We can do and be so much more than I think even you could have imagined. Everything has opened up for us and I pray that we will continue to climb this mountain long after our parents have become fatigued and fallen away. I pray that we will hold on to your teachings and make you proud as the father of the Mvusi clan. Although we do not know you, we still love you. It's because of you that we are the mighty people we have become. And I ask that you watch over us with each new generation that extends this family tree.

Dzanibe, Nqolo, Gaba - I thank you.

Your great granddaughter

Lwazi

The Sermon on Mount Mthekhala

by Simthembile Matyobeni

*When death is knocking it takes courage to ask 'Who's there?" but then to unwittingly say
"Come in!" takes blind audacity. Who said death knocks before entering? Death knocks
when already inside, just to notice others it has taken the one for whom it came.*

Oh, Mt. Mthekhala let me tell the sad story of the passing, the fall.
Oh, let the echoes replenish the dry winds that blow against your cold visage.
O, the fall, the death, the passing...
Isivivane obsequies have been laid to rest, the lone traveller has supplicated for
guidance.
Let him walk on the sterile road and not worry what lurks in its curves.
Long have the eyes been cast enkalweni, the heart buoyed on Ndiyanqwena's river,
where uMamlambo is enthroned.
Trystland waits afar to swallow uMlanjeni in its bosom.
We shan't wait for Nxele's return, for his homecoming is as a good as uNongqawuse.
The spoon shall never touch the foreskin, lest we insist that from aloe can spew out
honey.
Ntsikana woken from his deathbed by the honking of a Mazda 6.
Oh, how I envy Shaka's helicopter!
Let the boys holler jeers at water-shag, for their way is through grimy adornments...
Oh, Mt. Mthekhala, let my tongue fail to betray me.
Let uNtulo speak to me in my sleep and keep fastidious uLovane at bay, for when I saw
him chicken-pox nudged at me.
I became an avatar, the archetype that reigned as a polemicist of meagre significance.
Indeed, foolish sounds were made.
Let your will be done...
Mt. Mthekhala, forgive me for past misdeeds.
They were there before me.
They should have done something, instead of chasing after grasshoppers.
Blind oracles!
Victoria's tears tasted sweet and never cloy even today.
Let her cry everyday to quench their thirst.
Yet she will have none of their tears.
Her throat will be sore and her teeth will rot.
Oh, find it in your heart to forgive her.
Bowels always complained of why they always have to keep the faeces and the latter
complained why they should be chucked out of warmth.
Someone had sex with a dog, and hollered, "with intimation I've reached saturation
point!"
Husband's gonads chopped off, the wife shouted "let women's voice be heard!"
The whole fraternity cheered, "At least it's just an organ he lost, not his essence. He had
made her lose her essence. Viva! Viva! Let's chop off more penises! They don't matter
anyway! Semen-factory ready for in-vitro! Yee pee!"
"Comrades, pray hard! Many 4/5s are being lost. Get bars and lock those passion-
muscles away"...
Mt Mthekhala, I weep at your feet.

My Will
by Diana Stone

If I marry I will marry out of community of property.
If I make a child with Silvin that would be nice.
I not going to rush into marriage.
I like my freedom.
If I love Silvin the child is the bond and he will support me and the child.
I will stay by both houses.
The children must stay in both houses.
Silvin will stay in both houses.
The kids must feel secure in the houses.
They must finish school and go to university.
I must give most concentration to Silvin's feelings.
I am not going to be scarred for the future.
I keep on studying, noting and playing.
Go through psychology to get advice to work things good in my life.
Silvin will get all my belongings and the baby if there will be a baby.
I live everyday to the fullest.
I try to make people happy around me.
Life is about take and give.
It's to look beautiful, dress beautiful, drive your car.
Stay in your own home, feel good about yourself.
Apply for jobs to live a good life.
Don't be jealous of others
Give other people a try and don't put them down.
Try to appreciate.

End of story

TWEE GEDIGTE
van Marcelle Du Toit

respons op nietigverklaring van die siel

Klinkklaar
onder bleek neonlig
lê die landskap van die rede:
vrae hipoteses
voorlopig antwoorde

My herder, kreet ek
na watter dor weiveld lei jy my?
Uit watter brak poel moet ek drink?
Johannes van die Kruis se heimnisvolle nag
vir goed verby?
Wat vir 'n daeraad het dit verlig?

Dagraad van die rede sogenaamd
deur dowwe son verduister
in onbekende onverkende
uitwyke van tyd

Hoor my:
ek soek nie hel of hemel nie
geen engeltjies in nagrokkies
met vlerkies nie

Ek soek my sy siel se antwoord
op my siel se kreet om tydloosheid
wilde wulpse speelsheid
rymelary

ver buite rede se bereik

erns is groen

droef is stroef
swart sê hul
ek sê pers
aand wat nag word

luimigheid is wit en geel
oggend helder soos juweel
skoelappers dartel voëltjies
duik wip kweel

erns is groen
vrugbaar bewoë
soos die soen
van twee paar oë

TWO POEMS
by Jacob Kobina Ayiah Mensah

Joshua Tree

Remember the piled lights faintly floating

on the heated sand leaving

jostled stems, wet roots and dried leaves

in the deep grave month

April is dragging its weight

among many things to remember

I keep the fleeting glance

The Gun

At this early age of 103 my grandmother still carries her gun (a pistol,
hiding in her clothes) about in the house.
The gun is 81.
Though it's not functioned before,
it's now the first estates of her belongings.
They say it was giving to her by her grandmother,
who had carried it for so many years
unknown to her,
it's now ageless.

In the kitchen dressed like a nurse, she prepares
my morning tea with cakes and coffee,
it lives on the ebony table
closer to her life more than before.
Maybe she'll pull the trigger today.
Maybe she'll dust it after
slicing herself like lemons.
Maybe she'll call me back home
and teach me how to prepare its soapy water
for the regions down below the open window on my left.

Our neighbours in the house don't understand why she spends
long hours cooking for me and my mother.
when my wife lies in bed reading long novels.
Perhaps I'm the only grandson among her thirteen grandchildren.
Perhaps my mother is her only daughter among her five children
who was saved from the last rubble
when my only daughter and only child died
after seven days from birth.
Perhaps she's growing white
and she won't allow my wife
to touch me again.

Maybe I'm her gun.
Maybe I'm her eyes.
Maybe I'm her land,
she writes long letters
for we to return home.

She's measuring the size of the house
and prepares her soapy water.
she'll whitewash the stain walls with yellow paint.
I'll be the first grandson in that house,
I'll be her last grandson.
I'm her gun.
I'm her land.

Marothi
by Matete Malohle Motsoaledi

Maru go duša
a tla tswala ya matlakadibe
morethetho wa marothodi
le go ratha ga tladi
pele molalatladi
o ntšha nko morumong wa molala
monola o retšwela mohola
ra ikhola ka megoma

naga-tsotho ya re go kgolwa
ya tswala naga tala
tlala ya ba taaba tša botaala
ra palega dimpa re bina mokhora
makhura re tshotshoma
o široga diatla mošomo
dišego diphophoma

šeleo letebejane
le botoga hlogotlou
le lebile motsephiri
le tšhepile ka boso
phatleng le gadima tladi
le hupile marothi a bo matlakadibe
tsheola le bo kgogolamooko
kgomo di faretšwe ke bjo botala
mekaka e a gogoba

ntšhupetšeng melala ya babelegi
boMadiga le boMadingwaneng
Ke hlabe fase ka tša naka tsa marumo
ya ka ntwa ke hlabana ya mokhora
ke šila ka mehlagare lwaleng
šego tšešo di bjalo dithaba swiswi
la re go inola nko mebotong
wa bona go falala ga dienywa
tša melala ya bantendi

semponeng go sasanka
la nkhupela lehufa
le nthlolla lehu fa!
ga se nna
baitše ge o otla, o hlapaola ye mengwe

tsogelang mareneng
mmina thlanthlagane a le phare
ka hlogwana tsie ya mafiša
gape a ka se betle a le furaletše

le yona ya matlorotloro
baloi ga e ba tshetshole
monapelo ga a tsebje
ga bakwe kamoka ka ditsebe
ba bangwe ba ana tshele
ba re morwa'Madingoaneng le se mmone a le bjalo
o nameditšwe ke rena bo magana go phalwa
ge re rata re ka mo fegolla bjale ka sa borala
mampja a moruthula

moneša pula'matlorotloro
seaba marothi a mokhora
gopola sello sa tšhiololo
mokgoši wa mašuana
masetla'pelo tša makgwakgwa

se re go se kwa wa re se go bata ditsebe

re topeletse sa moeteng wa bo rraweno
le rena re bana beno
feta o tamiša ka keno
le rena re hlatswe meno

The Late Chief M
by JKS Makokha

Let us call him Mr Matchstick. Or Chief Matchstick for that was his official title. Or simply, Chief M.

I remember him very well although it has been eleven years since we last worked together. I had been commissioned by the government of a republic somewhere in Africa as an enumerator in the National Housing and Population Census process. The census has been conducted in this republic every ten years since 1949. The British colonial government, faced with an imminent war for independence by the natives, had thought it wise to find out actually how many heads and huts there were in the colony. These statistics would come in handy in case the restless natives made good their threat and rose in rebellion against the Crown. Of course, they did, but the British eventually won the long and dirty war in 1958. However, in spite of this resounding victory for the new Queen, the colony was lost in the winter of '63. The rest is history. The census endures. The recent one was conducted last year. The nation awaits the results. Some say they are still being (prepared) cooked or in local palaver: "The results are still in the kitchen".

For fourteen nights, Chief M and I had roamed the narrow slum paths of Location N., visiting homesteads under his dominion. There were one hundred and forty-four in total. Home after home; head after head. The process progressed smoothly albeit with minor hiccups. The seventy-four year old war veteran-turned-long serving chief, his crooked walking stick and I, ensured that the government got what it employed us to do - offer a comprehensive bilingual tabular of the total numbers of people and hovels under Chief Matchstick's jurisdiction. He had earned my admiration for his stamina and ability to explain some of the paranormal events and activities that spiced our joint exercise.

One of these occurrences stood out and makes him a memorable part of my history. So when I received an SMS from his office last Thursday that the poor old fellow had passed on, it is not the name but this past event that brought his face to my freezing mind on a street in downtown Berlin.

We had counted one hundred and seventeen homes and were proceeding at a steady pace. The North-western quarter of the location had been covered. People were highly cooperative. And this was part of the overall strategy: to start from the cooperative and Islamic quarters before proceeding to the animists - the latter still rebelled against ANY government effort to 'develop' their lives, in the same way their forefathers did against the Brits. They had not made it a secret that they would unleash all sorts of spirits, being the products of sorcery, on any khaki-dressed government fellow or his underling who appeared at their doorsteps carrying the flag of the ruling independence party and bearing the official government census ID. One normally docile chap had, in fact, erected a banner of iron sheet with the clear message written in jeep oil and faeces: NOWADAYS TO DIE IS EASY. ASK ME TO SHOW YOU JUST HOW. Of course, the message was in the widely-spoken urban slang, just in case....

The night of the memorable event, we had started from the abandoned butchery, by the old Hindu crematorium. A woman had given birth to quadruplets. She wanted us to count them immediately just in case one or two perished before the census was over. She had sent a powerful emissary: the new slum voodoo sorcerer, an unregistered refugee from DR Congo. We could not turn her request down, although it was not part of the plan for the night, so we proceeded off schedule and decided to count all the remaining graveyard quarters. So you will understand that most of the locals in this area were caught unawares as they were not prepared for us. They had thought we would only be with them two days hence per the schedule they had been given. No, not this night; no!

We entered the strange home of memory at exactly three and a half minutes to midnight. The pattern was the same: the chief walked ahead, I was always behind him at the recommended two feet distance. I was also usually armed with the voluminous scroll of fill-in-the-blank-spaces government spreadsheet protected by a plastic gunny sack. While on duty, the sack never left my head at all. Never. In it were other precious national materials bought dearly with tax-payer's money.

I had two kilos of pencils; ten grams of razor blades to help sharpen blunt pencils; a quarter kilo of Ever Ready batteries; and a pink plastic spotlight that took three batteries at a time. My over-size gumboots were heavy with black river mud stuck fast like demons on their soles. The left one was torn on the sole near the main toe and made a splotchy sound as I trudged behind the staggering old chief.

Presently, he started the now familiar introduction ritual given him by our pre-Census preparation workshop facilitator.

Chief M stood at military attention. So did I right behind him. He cleared his cancerous throat six times and in his croaky alto voice announced the arrival of His Excellency the Junior Officer of the Government of K National Housing and Population Census Exercise at homestead Number 119 of Ghetto G, Sub-location 55, of Location 715, of Division A/715, of District T/A/715, of Province W of the Republic of K, Africa, Earth!

He did this little preamble using a microphone powered by a jeep battery that he always carried in a canvas rucksack on his frail, bent back. He then hummed the first stanza of the national anthem as we stood waiting for the head of the homestead to tie or lock up his mongrels (or genies) that offered home security around these parts of the capital city.

Then came the silence. Silence. More silence.

The head of the homestead (lets call him Mr Y) came out, finally. He was armed with his bone-bladed scimitar, a shield made of bricks and cap with a miner's torch on its foreside. His naked body, clothed only in torn knickers, was painted with the colours of our flag. He proceeded with a small war dance, stabbing right and left in the air and yodeling in an archaic form of our vernacular. It went something like this:

"Horeeeeaa hai! Horrrraaaeee hia!" - repeated about seven or six times.

The chief whispered that I should dare not bolt away. His whisper came at a good time. We stood our ground. Mr Y jumped over his gate of broken beer bottles cemented together with asphalt and stood a metre above us in the air. Silence. More silence. More Silence. More Silence. More Silence. More Silence. Silence.

Then I found my voice. I first apologized for coming to his home unexpectedly, then courteously asked irate Mr Y if we could conduct our government business. All this time Chief M kept quiet. He just stood there smoking his marijuana from a wooden pipe and ignored the irate Mr Y.

Mr Y, a suspected hermaphrodite, came close to me. He opened the infant albino palm in his war pouch covered with cobwebs and let me smell the darkness in it. I did. With one raised eyebrow he looked straight into my bespectacled eyes. We understood each other. The pouch smelt of that alien plant without a name - the one we normally use in secret rites I cannot reveal here. I understood his war antics and urged the chief that we leave the good Mr Y.

Silence.

"We should come back tomorrow night or on a day specially set aside for his homestead," I reasoned, raising my voice to a loud whisper. Silence. Chief? Silence. ChieEEF!?? More silence.

Chief Matchstick only came around from his ganja reverie and recognized my presence after we had arrived at the next homestead. Panting, he exclaimed that I had counted the last homestead so fast!

"Remind me, young man, to include a paragraph on your persuasive and arithmetic skills in my letter of recommendation any time you need one from my good office," he said with a lop-sided smile.

*

I remember him now upon his death miles upon miles away from Location N. His eyes still bear in me that lost look they had on that night . . .

Iphupha

by Loyiso Lindani

Ndiphupha ndibaleka ndingenamngeni
Ndipholile, ndizolile, ingangeni ndawo
Ndawo ezolileyo enyangeni
Ndiphumelela emagqabini kule micelimngeni
Ndiphupha ndibhabha ndisemaweni
Sendagqitha ekuncumeleni oongantweni
Intliziyo yam sendayeka ukuyibeka exhaleni
Ndixhabasheka, ndingxamile ndisentweni
Ndiphupha kungasekho sijwili nasikhalo
Ukholo noyolo iyeyona nto ndiphila ngayo
Se lwabhubha usana olungubhubhane ugawulayo
Ndityala kuwo amasimi angenakukhula ukhula
Ndiphupha ndilusana ndisandul'ukuzalwa
Bonke bendibuka, intyatyambo esand'utyalwa
Iminwe enje ngemitha yelanga ethand'ukubhala
Ndiphupha ndisisibane, ndikhanyisela abo bathand'ukubhala

Mayakovsky
the new lyric hero
the socialist
revolutionary

by Jon Berndt

Mayakovsky among soldiers of the Red Army 1929.

Mayakovsky was born a woodcutters son in 1893, rose to become the poet of the Russian revolution in 1917 and then committed suicide in 1930 as Stalin came to power. He was a poet, artist and political agitator who produced some of the most inspirational and revolutionary art and literature of the early 20th century. He was dismissed in the West as 'the drummer of the Revolution' and criticised in the Soviet Union for being 'too influenced by avant garde modernism' then four years after his death he was canonised as a 'Socialist Realist' by Stalin. Yet his ghost still haunts those of us who would like to believe that revolutions can be both cultural and political. Like the ghost of Hamlet's father he speaks to us about love, art and politics – warning us about the dangers of surrogate fathers.

In order to appreciate Mayakovsky's poetry it is necessary to situate him in the context of the Russian 1917 Cultural Revolution and Futurism. The simultaneity of the political and cultural revolutions expressed itself in the conflict between artists and the Bolsheviks over who could claim to be the vanguard of the revolution. Both the leader of the Proletcult movement, Bogdanov, and Lenin the leader of the Bolsheviks, argued over who had the right to use the term avant garde .

•

The 1917 Cultural Revolution had its origins within the European modernist avant garde that was associated with revolutionary European political movements in the early 20th century. The borders between the emerging nation states in Europe remained badly policed well into the first quarter of the 20th Century and many of the European modernist artists moved back and forth between their respective countries with ease. The visual culture that developed went counter to the nationalist attempt to define national identities through the creation of national cultures. Internationalism was a widely shared ideal of both the political and cultural revolutionaries at the time. These cultural internationalists advocated a modernist break with the culture of the past while the respective parochial nationalists romanticised the pre-industrial past. Up until the late 1920s in Russia, during the first five-year-period, the internationalism of the German and Russian *modernists* created what became known as the 'two Berlins' ; Berlin and Petrograd were the epicentres of the Russian cultural revolution.

While the Italian artist and poets were laying the foundations for Futurism Russia was going through its 1905 Revolution that was to be the moment of political awakening for Mayakovsky. Mayakovsky's description of this formative moment in his life described it in predominantly visual terms 'I saw it in terms of painting anarchists in black, Socialist Revolutionaries in red, Social Democrats in dark-blue and the federalists in other colours.' In *I Myself* he says he 'read voraciously' and was 'impressed for the rest of (his) life by the socialists' ability to disentangle facts and systematize the world … (he) was introduced to a Marxist circle and began to consider (himself) a Social-Democrat.'

Mayakovsky started out as a political activist and propagandist for the Russian Social Democratic Party spending three periods in prison between the years 1908 to 1910. When he was finally released he devoted himself to his poetry and art because like other revolutionary artists of his time he believed that his poems and posters were in-themselves works of political agitation. In his own words he wanted 'to create socialist art' in the belief that his work would contribute to the building of a socialist world. Gorky's criticism of Mayakovsky for being too ego-centric failed to grasp the extent of the merger of the personal and political in his work. It is precisely because this combination of the political and personal that his lyrics speak to us today. We realize with hindsight that one of the problems with socialism in the 20th century was the extent to which it obliterated the personal for the sake of the collective. Mayakovsky's great contribution was his fervent personal commitment to socialism expressed in a modern lyric style shaped by avant guard art of the early 20th century. He was both a cultural and a political iconoclast using new lyrics to build a new world.

Roman Jacobson, the Russian linguist, literary critic, and fellow early Russian Modernist summed up the spirit of the time:

We strained toward the future to impetuously and avidly leave any past behind us. The links in the chain of time were broken. We lived too much in the future, thought about it, believed in it, the self-generating evils of the day did not exist for us. We lost a sense of the present. We were the witnesses and participants in the great socialist, scientific, and other catacysms.

•

Mayakovsky's association with the continental modernist movements starts with Futurism that had its origins in Italy. In 1909 the poet Marinetti produced the first Futurist manifesto which established the Italian Futurist movement. Italian artists Umberto Boccioni and Carlo Cara combined the new painting technique known as *divisionism* (a style of painting in small dots similar to French *Pointillism*) with modern pictorial forms calling it Futurist art. Their paintings such as **Funeral of the Anarchist Galli** and **The City Rises** in 1910-11 were a response to the general strike of 1904 and anticipated the radicalism of the Biennio Rosso (two red years) of the mass factory occupations of 1920 when half a million workers took over and ran the factories in the cities of Milan and Turin. Their initial contribution to the breaking of the constricting confines of 19th century culture 'in order to exploit the resources of the imagination' (Apollonio 1973) had a profound influence on culture throughout Europe. The Futurists' tour to the major cities of the continent spread these ideas as far a field as Moscow and Petrograd.

There are many similarities between the work of the Italian and Russian artists at this time which gave rise to new pictorial forms such as the red wedge shape in Russolo's Revolt and Lissitsky's **Beat the Whites with the Red Wedge**. In Russolo's painting the red wedge is made up of abstracted figures storming the ridged geometrical structure of buildings. Lissitsky's painting only used abstract non figurative shapes it communicates a range of ideas about the civil war period of the Russian Revolution. Both depict the revolution as a red wedge battering its way into the conservative structures of the bourgeois world.

However, while Russian Futurists were also cultural iconoclasts they distanced themselves from the Italian Futurists. "The Russian Futurists definitively broke with the poetic imperialism of Marinetti, having earlier booed him during his visit to Moscow (1913)." (the LEF Programme 1923). The Russian artists were keen to stake their claim on their own form of Futurism. Instead of celebrating war as the agent of social change the Russians staked their claim on revolution as the doorway to the future. They 'drowned out the saber-rattling of the war-signers' and wrote their own manifesto called **A Slap in the Face of Public Taste** in 1913. In **I Myself** Mayakovsky wrote about how, 'After several nights, the lyric poets gave birth to a joint manifesto … and so brought out **A Slap in the Face of Public Taste**'.

A Slap in the Face of Public Taste

by d. burliuk, alexander kruchenykh, v. mayakovsky, victor khlebnikov 15th december 1913

To the readers of our New First Unexpected.

We alone are the face of our Time. Through us the horn of time blows in the art of the word.

The past is too tight. The Academy and Pushkin are less intelligible than hieroglyphics.

Throw Pushkin, Dostoevsky, Tolstoy, etc., etc. overboard from the Ship of Modernity.

He who does not forget his first love will not recognize his last.

Who, trustingly, would turn his last love toward Balmont's perfumed lechery? Is this the reflection of today's virile soul?

Who, faintheartedly, would fear tearing from warrior Bryusov's black tuxedo the paper armorplate? Or does the dawn of unknown beauties shine from it?

Wash Your hands which have touched the filthy slime of the books written by those countless Leonid Andreyevs.

All those Maxim Gorkys, Kuprins, Bloks, Sologubs, Remizovs, Averchenkos, Chornys, Kuzmins, Bunins, etc. need only a dacha on the river. Such is the reward fate gives tailors.

From the heights of skyscrapers we gaze at their insignificance!...

We order that the poets' rights be revered:

- To enlarge the scope of the poet's vocabulary with arbitrary and derivative words (Word-novelty).
- To feel an insurmountable hatred for the language existing before their time.
- To push with horror off their proud brow the Wreath of cheap fame that You have made from bathhouse switches.
- To stand on the rock of the word "we" amidst the sea of boos and outrage.

And if for the time being the filthy stigmas of your "Common Sense" and "Good Taste" are still present in our lines, these same lines for the first time already glimmer with the Summer Lightning of the New Coming Beauty of the Self-sufficient (self-centered) Word.

•

The split between the Italian and Russian Futurists was but one anomaly in a complex and varied movement that in its initial phase expressed conflicting ideas combining Italian Nationalism with revolutionary socialism. Consequently many commentators failed to see this complexity and dismissed the Futurists as mere Fascists. failing to appreciate how in its early days its iconoclasm won the support of the Italian workers who also wanted to destroy bourgeois society. We know that Gramsci wrote a column, Marinetti the Revolutionary in the socialist paper L'Ordine Nuovo (The New Order) in 1921 in which he praised the Futurists:

When they supported the Futurists, the workers' groups showed that they were not afraid of destruction, certain as they were of being able to create poetry, paintings and plays, like the Futurists: these workers were supporting historicity, the possibility of a proletarian culture created by the workers themselves.

The Italian Fascists were equally impressed by this iconoclastic modernity so when they set out to portray Fascism as new and modern they co-opted Futurism into Mussolini's cultural fair in 1933. The Fascists were keen to portray their 1922 coop d'état known as the March on Rome (Marcia su Roma) not only as moment when they came to power but also as a clean break with the past. It was a simple matter for the Italian

Fascism to aestheticise its politics by buy co-opting artists and poets who celebrated war instead of revolution.

Mayakovsky on the other hand started his own brand of Futurism and redefined the poet as the new lyric hero – the socialist revolutionary. It was a Futurism that took lyric poetry beyond the limited expression of the thoughts and feelings of the poet into the thick of revolutionary action.

What About You 1913

> I splashed some colours from a tumbler
> and smeared the drab world with emotion.
> I charted on a dish of jelly
> the jutting cheekbones of the ocean.
> Upon the scales of a tin salmon
> I read the calls of lips yet mute.
> And you,
>   could you have played a nocturne
> with just a drainpipe for a flute?

After this tentative start with a series of short poems like *What About You* Mayakovsky wrote his long poem *The Cloud in Pants*. Written in four parts it touched on revolution, love, religion and art. In 1915 he met Lily Brik with whom he fell in love and had an unrequited affair until 1928. She featured as the femme fatale in *Cloud in Pants* and many of his later poems which, together with *The Backbone Flute, War and the World* and *Man*, established his reputation.

The Cloud in Pants (extract) 1915
(adapted from the Russian by Augustus Young, ARS INTERPRES 2005)

> Big Shots,
> I promise to embolise
> your expense-account complacency
> with a clot from the infractions
> of a broken heart,
> and to state
> brash youthful
> disregard when gangrene
> sets in
> I won't wait
> for grey hairs
> and worldly cares
> to soften my views.

While *Cloud in Pants* is very typical of his early period, his poems like *Order of the Day to the Army of the Arts* and his work on the ROSTA agit-prop posters, define his middle period. This period marks a high point in his work when he was able to weave together his poetry, his art and his politics. He developed the ROSTA hand painted posters for the Russian Telegraph Service. At the time of the civil war (some times referred to as the period of War Communism) there were acute shortages and limited means of communicating in a very large country. Mayakovsky worked to overcome these problems of scarcity and distance by hand painting posters then putting them on trains to be transported throughout Russia where they were pasted up in the windows of the ROSTA offices along the rail system. In 1920 he described his work as, 'Days and nights at ROSTA. ... I write and draw. Have done about three thousand posters and about six thousand captions.' In the Lef Program Mayakovsky asserts that 'we produced the first real works of art of the October epoch ...' and yet they 'did not indulge in aesthetics, producing works for our own pride. The experience which we had attained was put to use creating agitational-artistic works which the revolution demanded (ROSTA posters, newspaper feuilletons, etc.)'.

The Russian Futurists were never really accepted by the Bolsheviks so they were forced to agitate for their own ideas which they did by producing the newspaper Art of the Commune as well as touring the 'factories and plants to stage discussions and readings'. In Mayakovsky's view, 'Our ideas won over the workers' audience' in the 1920s. Prior to this he had travelled extensively in the period of war communism doing public readings of his poems to the soldiers fighting the civil war. These soldiers not only provided a ready and captive audience for Mayakovsky's poetry readings, but also other agit-prop theatrical productions. The soldiers of the Red Army were used as participants in the great mass spectacles of 1920/21 to celebrate the revolution (like those when Tatlin's monument, *The Monument to the 3rd International,* was carried through the streets) and for large crowd scenes in films like Potemkin and Ten Days that Shook the World. While cynics may despair that this constituted a manipulation of culture it nevertheless provided the soldiers with the opportunity to become active participants in the 1917 cultural revolution.

Order of the Day to the Army of the Arts (extract) (1918)

Slam!
Bang!
Crash!
No fun
To tinker at factories,
Your face in coke-soot smearing,
And then after work, at another's luxury
To blink, with eye balls bleary.
Enough of penny worth truths!
Old trash from your hearts erase!
Streets for paint-brushes we'll use,
Our palettes – squares with their wide-open space.
Revolution's days have yet to be sung
by the thousand page book of time.
Into the streets, the crowds among,
futurists,
drummers,
masters of rhyme!

This poem expresses some of the core sentiments of the 1917 Cultural Revolution; the break with the past (old trash), the transposition of art from the easel into life (the streets and squares) and the fundamental identification with the social revolution.

One of Mayakovsky's first recollections of painting concepts was his memory of the humorous supplement of the magazine Rodina (Homeland). His father was a subscriber and Mayakovsky claims that, 'The cartoons are discussed and waited for.' These early memories shaped his visual approach to his agit prop posters that consisted of a series of visual images and captions very much in the a cartoon style. Latter during the NEP period when he designed adverts with his fellow Productivists, his cigarette poster The Best Nipple employed a humorous style that subverted the advertisment.

During the New Economic (NEP) period limited capitalism was allowed back into Russia and Mayakovsky along with his fellow artists and poets struggled to fit into what they regarded as the art of capitulation. Capitalism (all be it in a limited form) was re-introduced by the Bolsheviks as they struggled to rebuild Russia after the period of War Communism. Not only did the Bolsheviks re-introduce capitalist economic planning but they cut state funding to the arts forcing many artist like Mayakovsky and Rodchenko to design advertising for the new petit bourgeoisie known as NEPs. He was very active in Lef (a radical modernist group of artists and writers) and worked closely with the Productivist artist Rodchenko during the NEP period.

The cultural revolutionaries, Tatlin, Rodchenko, Lisitsky, Mayakovsky, Rozanova and Stepanova in their own way were committed to an artistic utilitarianism that attempted to build a new proletarian culture. This was strongly asserted by the Productivists redefinition of the artist as a producer that not only challenged old ideas about art but in the reconstruction period of the 1920s positioned the artist as an 'engineer' who's task it was to change the world.

Unprepared to completely capitulate to the NEPs and become the window dressers of the new petit bourgeoisie Mayakovsky and his associates tried to reconfigure Futurism/Constructivism into Productivism and join the workers in the building of socialism in Russia. They designed workers overalls, workers libraries and canteens and every day objects like textiles and tea pots. Mayakovsky attacked the market driven philistinism of the new party autocrat with his ***Talking with the Taxman about Poetry*** published in 1926.

It should be born in mind that we only have a partial rendition of Mayakovsky's poem. Although we have lost some of the visual word play of the original Cyrillic typography the translation retains the word and line spacing that establishes a rhythm and makes the poem into a typographic image. In his ***How are Verses Made*** he wrote that 'the way lines are divided is … dictated by the necessity of hammering home the rhythm'. The visual typography, the visual shape of the words and lines is crucial for understanding both the meaning and the rhythm of the poem (note I have placed the poems in frames/boxes so that they are separated from the text of this paper. Ideally they should be seen on a page by themselves).

Talking with the Taxman about Poetry (*extract*) 1926

As of right
            I'm
                        demanding a place
with workers
            and peasants
                                    of the poorest sort.
But if
            you think
                        all I do is just Press
Words other people use
                        into my service,
Comrades,
            come here,
                                    let me give you my pen
and you
            can yourselves
                                                write your own verses!

For appreciation of the visuality of Myakovsky's poetry I have reproduced an extract from his 1926 poem **To Sergey Esenin.**

If a Party man
            had been given the chore
                                    of watching
That your main stress
                        was on content,
You'd have written
                        every day
                                    lines
                                    by the score

The modernism of the Russian avant-garde, which merged the cultural and the political, had a very brief period within the imagination of the Russian Socialist Revolution. Barely three years after the Bolshevik revolution, the belief that socialism was the road to a new world order suffered its most cataclysmic blow with the failure of the Germans to carry through a revolution in their country. Socialist culture turned its eyes from the future and the past became the measure of all things, the great spectacles became celebrations of the dead. The building of the new world ceased and the dead were resurrected as a way of defining a national culture. Socialist culture became Socialist Realism, an unreal realism of cardboard bureaucrats as the Party assumed the task of building socialism for the workers by decree from the balcony of the Kremlin. Gone were the large captivated audiences of soldiers and the mass spectacles of the period of War Communism. Instead of cheering soldiers Mayakovsky was confronted by students who interrupted his poetry readings and shouted him off the stage in 1930. It was clear that the lyric hero of the revolution no longer had any currency in the unreality of Socialist Realism which needed unreal men and women for the great five year plans to work.

Mayakovsky retreated into a room to talk to the ghost of Lenin in 1929 and then committed suicide in 1930. His funeral re-enacted the mass spectacles of 1920/21 with a procession and ceremony of 30,000 people, and the designer of the Monument to the 3rd International, Tatlin designed the catafalque that carried Mayakovsky's body through the streets of Moscow.

Why he shot himself is not clear as he did not leave a suicide note to explain his last act. His fellow Futurist, Roman Jacobson, maintained that Mayakovsky suffered from a particularly Russian form of depression which he called byt – a virtually untranslatable Russian word that includes concepts such 'Philistinism, the commonplace and the daily grind …' (Jacobson 1967). Mayakovsky had suffered periods of depression throughout his life, linked to his unrequited love for Lily Brik, the failure of the cultural revolution and finally the rejection of his work by the 1930's generation of Socialist Realists. His poem Conversation with Comrade Lenin published in 1929 expresses his alienation from the politics of NEP period barely five years after the death of Lenin.

Conversation With Comrade Lenin *(extract)* 1929
(Translated by Irina Zheleznova, Progress Publshers 1975)

They strut around
                    as proudly
                                        as peacocks,
badges and fountain pens
                            studding their chests.
We'll lick the lot of 'em –
                    but,
                            to lick 'em
is no easy job
                at the very best
On snow-covered lands
                                        and stubby fields
in smokey plants
                and on factory sites
with you in our hearts,
                        Comrade Lenin,
                                                    we build,
we think,
    we breathe,
                    we live,
                            and we fight!"
Awhirl with events,
                    packed with jobs one too many,
the day slowly sinks
                    as the night shadows fall.
There are two in the room:
                            I
                            and Lenin –
a photograph
                on the wall.

References

Mayakovsky,V. *How are Verses Made?* Jonathan Cape London 1970

Mayakovsky,V. *Vladimir Mayakovsky Selected Workers in Three Volumes. Vol 1*. Raduga Publishers 1985

Williams R. *Means of Communication as Means of Production Problems in Materialism and Culture*. Verso (1980).

Benjamin W. The Author as Producer written in Germany during the 1920s.

Filippov A. *Production Art*. Bann S Ed. Thames and Hudson 1974.

Jakobson, R. *The Generation That Squandered Its Poets*. (Excerpts) Dale E, Peterson. Yale French Studies No.39 Literature and Revolution (1967) pp. 119-125

Foot notes

1.   *The Russian 1917 Cultural Revolution took place simultaneously with the October 1917 Russian Revolution and led to the formation of the Proletcult movement which had over half a million members. After following a period cultural tolerance the Bolsheviks closed down Proletcult in 1921.*

2.   *vangard/avant-garde From the French military term avant-garde to refer to the leading edge of the army - a small force sent out in front to surprise the enemy. Marx himself never used the term. Lenin coined the phrase when he wrote What is to be done in 1905 - and in fact he used the French term :avant-garde". The use of the term was further confused because many European languages do not distinguish between the two. The fact that groups of artists used the term in very much the same sense that Lenin did - the Proletkult used the term when describing their call for a cultural revolution.*

3.   *Clark, K. Petersburg Crucible of Cultural Revolution. Harvard University Press 1996*

4.   *I Myself .Translated by Alex Miller. Mayakovsky V. Selected Verse. Raduga Publishers (1985)*

5.   *The Generation That Squandered Its Poets. (Excerpts) Roman Jakobson: Dale E, Peterson. Yale French Studies No.39 Literature and Revolution (1967) pp. 119-125*

6.   *'The lyric poem is the most personal and private of the literary genres. Yet in the 20th century many lyric poems are social in nature, recording the consequences for individuals of institutional injustice and brutality.' Gutman H. "Identity, Relevance, Text: Reviewing English Studies" at Calcutta University on February 8, 2001.*

7.   *There are some interesting theoretical echoes in Walter Benjamin's The Author as Producer written in Germany during the 1920s*

8.   *cat·a·falque n. A raised and decorated platform on which the coffin of a distinguished person lies in state before or during a funeral*

The Fate Of Revolutionary Poets
by Allan Kolski Horwitz

What would you be doing if you lived today?

you would still be drinking vodka
                              smoking heavily
sighing when a new version of Lily
                              sheds her white petals and stands before you
aglow in your adoration
                    evading your desperate hands

you would still be working
                         designing posters for strikes and demonstrations
because power remains too much to handle
                    those who have taken the helm in their grasping hands
don't know how to steer between reefs
                         the daily grind mashes their galley slaves

you would still be walking at night
                              in the snow or the rain
asking why walls are being built
                         not for houses of knowledge and feeling
but for prisons and sweatshops

you would still be trying to reach out
                         despite the clamour of brands and tweets
 movie car chases
                    hijackings
                         serial celebrities on the rampage
bank bailouts
            nuclear blowouts
those without means
                    and those who squander them
                                   drowning in the swirling tides

you would still be jumping up
                              when words stick together
you would still be a celebrant
                         bearing the seal of conviction
you would still have some flame flicker
                         when a site of beauty unveils amazement

indeed comrade poet
                    you would not be alone
lamenting the failed revolution
                              love
        you are not alone

TWO POEMS
by Mandy Mitchell

After midnight, waking feverish, sinking

After midnight, waking feverish, sinking
back into deep sleep. My dead night punctuated,
at last, by dreams. Here you are.
You tell me the story of your life,
and I am concurrently with you in your places.
I am in your life. Seated before heavy curtains,
you show me your homes, your lands. Places I know
but have never seen. And then we travel further,
another continent, a high mountain village
where the women wear henna on their hands
and beads on their bodies. It is cold.
They are your spaces, but they are familiar.
There are silent words between us
And I tell myself that this is not real; it is only a dream.
Then there you are, close to me, your life a book
which you offer to me. I turn the pages
filled with your stories, your pictures.
The last entry is in my handwriting,
an unfinished poem; my scribbles, my notes, still there.

Driving home after a Sunday spent at the mall

Driving home after a Sunday spent at the mall,
feeling nauseous from the fluorescent lighting
and air conditioning; frustrated from trying to fill the gap.
Rain falls cold as snow; headlights blinding in our eyes.
The atmosphere, saturated with resentment,
is exaggerated by the unforgiving evening.
We hurl words hard as rocks at one another,
and then lose ourselves in those silent places.
Back at home we both know that the bed
will be cold; I'll turn my back
and reach for my copy of Anna Karenina.

To Keep A Long Story Short
by Mphutlane wa Bofelo

This is the story she always wants to tell. She has carried this story with her everywhere. Bits and pieces of this story are scattered all over Limpopo. The details are hidden in some room or any other space she's inhabited at one time or another. The gruelling, heavy details are known by every wall she's talked to. The screams are hidden in every song she could have sung if whenever she opened her lips she did not have a lump in the throat. The lyrics are in every sigh, in every smile, in every step . . . despite the load. Just watch her face when she sings with Miriam Makeba: "Gauteng; banna ba rona ba shwetse komponeng kwana Gauteng". Look at her eyes each time Hugh Masekela's Stimela is playing: "There is a train…"

These songs take her into the hearts and minds of the mineworkers and hostel dwellers; men who wake at dawn to face being swallowed by the shaken earth, and return every evening to the filth and stink of communal toilets and showers. They fill her nostrils with the smell of carbon, sorghum beer, marijuana, sheep's head, urine, sweat, muti and vomit piled together tight. She imagines herself eating while a few centimetres away someone is 'phalazing'. And behind the curtain some sex-starved fellows have resorted to DIY or to exchanging pounds; or some old man is groaning and breathing heavily on top of a hungry girl or boy smuggled in from the township. She has always taken the death of men in the compounds that Makeba sings about literally. Not for a moment did she think of it as an emotional death.

•

It is always very difficult to deal with the death of a husband; or having to take care of a husband dying from tuberculosis; or to watch a stroke snatch your uncle within a week of him returning from the big lights. But nothing surpasses the anguish and torment of a husband who is there but not there. During the first week of his return (after so many months!), you think he is still dealing with his demons. You rationalise that in a matter of time his soul will return from the fatiguing working conditions in the mines, the brutalising living conditions in the hostels, the harsh struggle that is city life - and come back to the simple and humble, but humane, life of the village. A month later you feel there something in the house killing the spirit. You turn the furniture around, burn incense, change the flowers regularly and increase the number of prayers. After six months, when the feeling grows heavier, you start to think there is something wrong with you. You change lip-gloss, buy new lingerie, wear shorts, return to the mini-skirt, tighten your cleavage, and start working on your moves. One year and six months later you decide 'the wrong' is actually inside you; or maybe inside both of you. You buy him men's magazines and yourself women magazines. You take turns in reading them. Sometimes you read the articles aloud to each other. You read motivation and spiritual journals. You both enrol at a gymnasium. You decide to give yoga a chance. It's difficult to find these things in Thohoyandou. You actually drive long hours to satisfy these longings. Sometimes you fly somewhere/anywhere for a change of environment. But you arrive at the same cold atmosphere and blame it on jet-leg. Two years later, he's checked for diabetes and there's nothing wrong. You've done your bit. Not even your sweet kisses and hot lips or your tongue-ring succeeds to make it rise up. You have hopped from psychiatrist to sex-therapist to sangoma and have tried everything from herbs to meditation to dhikr and tawiz. You no longer have a religion or culture. Anything that will help is welcome.

There will be disorder in the way this story is told. Don't blame it on me. I am not the author. I am just a ghost writer. This is the story she always wanted to tell but every time she put pen to paper her fingers froze; and every time she opened her mouth she felt a lump in her throat. This story shows that perhaps therapy is better when it is informal, located in every day activity rather than in some institution. In this case Masingita found that she felt better each time she cleared her mind and vented her feelings in the disguise of a 'status update' on facebook and Blackberry messages. The update she put on the Miriam Makeba and Hugh Masekela songs – and the feelings they evoke in her – invited three hundred comments from individuals and collectives as varied as bishops and pawnshops, teachers and preachers, philosophers, doctors, drunkards, ex-cons, CEO's and opportunists like me. After several inboxes on facebook, and more conversations via BBM, she finally accepted my advice to join the Elephant Jazz Club – of which I am a founder. I had told her that jazz is the clinic of the mind and nourishment for the soul. I had the double-agenda of increasing the female membership of my club and of becoming her comforter. It was only after several jazz sessions - and some sessions better left unmentioned here - that the third ulterior motive kicked in. The more Masingita opened up to me, the more I realised that hers is a story that needs to be told. I've never written a story before. My writing skills are so bad that I've not even tried poetry despite the fact that these days a few lines about love, sex and 'how beautiful is our country' can make you a pop star - something I've always (secretly) yearned to be. But knowing that my chances of being a singer are naught, having failed miserably at the dance academy, and my fame as a jazz fundi being limited to the 'borders' of Limpopo, I just convinced myself that telling Masingita's story was my only chance to be the New Great Thing. Of course, there may be a problem with parts of the story where I begin to feature prominently. My wife is an avid reader, you know.

Come omniscient narrator; take the story forward!

Abe and Masingita don't know how it happened. They have made it a point to play it safe all the time. But these things happen. And time does not stand in one place nor does it turn back. In a few months the signs will begin to show and people will start asking questions. She had confided to both her aunt-in-law and her mother that she and Alfonso have not known each other since his return from Welkom where he had been working over the past few months. Both empathised with her as they knew that the problem was not with her. What they did not know was eating the heart and head of Alfonso making it difficult for him to know her again after this long period of separation. Still Masingita feels a sense of betrayal. Her husband is truly getting sicker by the day. The way she sees it, his sunken eyes and daily weight loss speak of unbearable emotional trauma - or perhaps the person who bewitched him has since passed on to the Other Life. The alarm bell only rings the minute he starts having unstoppable diarrhoea and vomiting endlessly. She is also beginning to vomit. The doctor recommends that they both undergo medical tests. Her HIV result is negative. His is positive. Her pregnancy results are positive.

Watsenjiswa Emadlelo Laluhlata
by Mduduzi Shongwe

Nangabe usafundza uye ucabange kutsi nasewucedzile sikolwa lonkhe live liyobe selisetandleni takho. Uye utitjele kutsi konkhe lotsandza kukwenta ekuphileni kuyokwenteka, kuphela-nje nasewucedzile sikolwa. NaPhetsile bekacabanga kanjalo. Kodvwa lokwenteka kuye kwamfundzisa kutsi kufundza sikolwa ute usicedze kumane kusicalo sendlela lendze yekutsi uyoba yini ekuphileni. Kucedza sikolwa akusiso siphetfo sendlela leya emphumelelweni, kodvwa kumane kusicalo sayo. Nemaphutsa longawenta nangabe sewucedze sikolwa angatsintsa nobe ashintje lonkhe likusasa lakho.

BekunguLwesine ekuseni. Bantfu bebagcwele banyatselana emakethe kaManzini, kulaseSwatini. Kulemakethe kulapho kutsengiswa khona imisebenti yetandla lesuka etindzaweni letehlukahlukene. Kukhona labesuka eMaputo labatotsengisa lapha emakethe kaManzini kantsi futsi kukhona nalabesuka eGauteng bona batocupha umsebenti wetandla lotsengiswa lapha kute bayowutsengisa eGoli. NaPhetsile bekatfunywe nguBabekati wakhe ngalelilanga kutsi atomtsengisela umsebenti wakhe wetandla. Kulapha lapho ahlangana khona naDuduzile Mazibuko labetibita ngekutsi ungusisi Dudu, lobuya eGauteng, labekete kutocupha umsebenti wetandla kute ayowutsengise eGoli.

Duduzile bekabonakala angumuntfu lomsikati lonenhlitiyo lenhle nalotsandzako kusita lomunye umuntfu. Kantsi bekayimpisi leyebhetse sikhumba semvu futsi bekathandza kudlalela kubantfu lokubonakala sengatsi abanalo lwati lolukahle ngetintfo. Njengobe bekahambahamba abuka tintfo letitsengiswako, wanela kufika kuPhetsile wabe asambuta kutsi tonkhe letintfo takhe labetiphetse tingambita malini nangabe angamtsengisela tona tonkhe kanye kanye. Watsi kubalabala Phetsile wabe asamtjela kutsi setitonkhe tingambita emakhulu lamabili nemashumi lasihlanu emarandi. Wanela kuva leyomali wabe asatsi ucela kutsi atitsatse atiyise emotweni yakhe kute atomkhokhela imali yato tonkhe.

Banele kufika emotini bafaka timphahla wase uyamkhokhela emakhulu lamabili nemashumi lasihlanu emarandi. Phetsile wabonga wagangadza kwatise phela kutsi nyalo bekasacedzile kutsengisa ngalelolanga njengobe tintfo takhe bese tisheshe taphela ekuseni kangaka. Ngaphambi kwekutsi behlukane babese bayacoca khona lapho emotweni, kwaba kucoca kwebantfu labatsandza kwatana kancono. Kulapho naPhetsile atfola khona litfuba lekutsi atjele Duduzile ngako konkhe kuhlupheka kwakhe. Wamtjela kutsi usandza kucedza matekuletjeni nekutsi bekafuna umsebenti kodvwa wangawutfola, kungako nyalo bekasatsengisela Babekati wakhe lomsebenti wetandla lapha emakethe.

Duduzile wabonisa kuvelana naye kodvwa wabese umtjela kutsi yena abengamsita ngemsebenti nangabe angaya eGoli ngobe khona kunematfuba lamanyenti emsebenti. Waphindze wametsembisa nekutsi nematfuba ekutfola umsebenti nesemaveni langesheya kwetilwandle abamanyenti nangabe sewuseGoli, njengobe yena anebantfu labatiko labafunelana umsebenti emaveni langesheya kwetilwandle.

Tamjabulisa kakhulu letindzaba Phetsile, lokukuphela kwenkinga laba nayo kwaba kutsi abengenaye umuntfu langaya kuyohlala kakhe lena eGoli nekutsi bekangenato tincwadzi tekuhamba aphumele ngaphandle kwelive lakubo laseSwatini. Duduzile wamane watsi akangatikhatsati ngaloko kunaloko akasale acabanga ngalendzaba bese baphindze bayahlangana ngaLwesine wekucala enyangeni letako kute batocedzela indzaba yabo nangabe awufuna mbamba umsebenti.

Phetsile wehlukana naDuduzile ajabule kakhulu futsi nyalo bekasabona kutsi sengatsi utotfola emadlelo laluhlata nangabe angaphumelela kutsi aye eGoli. Nanobe Duduzile bekabonakala angumake losacinile, kodvwa kutibita kwakhe ngekutsi ungusisi Dudu ngesikhatsi atetfula kuPhetsile akuzange kumkhatsate kakhulu loko ngobe wacabanga kutsi njengemuntfu waseGoli kungenteka kutsi unguloluhlobo lwemuntfu lolutitjela kutsi phela 'kuguga lotsandzako.' Watsi nobe Phetsile asaphikelela ngekumbita ngekutsi ungumake Mazibuko, ngobe lulwimi lwakhe belungakwetayele kubita umuntfu lomdzala ngeligama, kodvwa wamekhuta watsi kuncono abombita ngekutsi ungusisi Dudu.

Phetsile wefika ekhaya kuBabekati wakhe angawuvali umlomo ngemuntfu lonemusa longaka labehlangene naye emakethe kaManzini. Wamcocela konkhe lobekwenteke emakethe futsi wamtjela nangematfuba emsebenti labewatsenjiswe nguDuduzile waseGoli. Nanobe Babekati wakhe angakujabulelanga kakhulu kutsi Duduzile ungumuntfu waseGoli, kodvwa kute lakungako labengakusho kwekumvimba ekubeni angawabambi lawomatfuba emsebenti ngobe vele bebatihluphekela kantsi nematfuba ekutfola umsebenti abengabonwa eSwatini. Noko wamecwayisa ngekutsi abocaphela ngobe abengamati phela naloyo Duduzile futsi wamcela kutsi nobe ngabe angate awutfole umsebenti khona lena eGoli kodvwa angabokhohlwa kutiphatsa kahle, lokuyimfundziso labemkhulise ngayo.

Intfo labeyimangalisa kutsi naloyo Duduzile akazange atikhatsate kangako ngesikhatsi Phetsile amtjela kutsi akanato tincwadzi tekuphuma eSwatini aye eveni lelingaphandle futsi akazange atikhatsate kangako nangalesikhatsi amtjela kutsi akanaso sihlobo lasatiko eGoli langasivakashela kute abe sedvute nalendzawo yaseGoli lenemisebenti leminyenti. Lokukuphela kwentfo Duduzile layigcizelela kuPhetsile kutsi akacabange ngalendzaba bese uyamtjela ngaLwesine weliviki lekucala lenyanga letako nangabe awufuna mbamba umsebenti. Naye-ke Phetsile akukho lokungako lakwenta kwekulungisa tincwadzi temvume yekuhamba aphumele ngaphandle kwelaseSwatini ngobe nangu naDuduzile abebonakala angakhatsatekile kangako ngaloko.

Wefika Lwesine weliviki lekucala lenyanga Phetsile labe avumelene ngalo kutsi utohlangana naDuduzile emakethe kaManzini. Nangalelilanga Phetsile bekaphetse umsebenti wetandla wakaBabekati wakhe labetowutsengisa khona lapho emakethe kute atokwati nekutsi ahlangane naDuduzile. Watfola Duduzile sekukadze amlindzele khona lapho emakethe. Batsi ngekubingelelana wase utsi akatsatse wonkhe umsebenti wetandla labetowutsengisa awuyise emotweni yakhe kute atomtsengela wona wonkhe kanye kanye. Watsi nakawubala Phetsile lomsebenti wetandla labewuphetse ngalelilanga watfola kutsi ubita likhulu nemashumi lasihlanu emarandi. Duduzile wamkhokhela yonkhe imali yawo base batsi kuhlala kancane emotweni yaDududzile kute bacoce ngalendzaba yekufuna kwakhe umsebenti.

Kute lokunyenti Phetsile labengakusho ngalelilanga ngaphandle kwekutsi waciniseisa Duduzile kutsi uwudzinga mbamba lomsebenti nanobe-ke angenato tincwadzi tekuhamba aphume kulaseSwatini nekutsi akanaye umuntfu langaya kuyohlala kakhe lena eGoli kute abesedvutane nalomsebenti. Kuko konkhe loku Duduzile watsi kufanele angakhatsateki ngako ngobe utomlungisela yonkhe intfo futsi utometfwalela tonkhe tindleko taloko.

Phetsile wabonga kwate kwaphela emagama ngalomusa longaka Duduzile labetsi utomentela wona kodvwa wase uyabuta kutsi uyomkhokhela kanjani nangabe asasebenta ngako konkhe loku lamentele kona. Duduzile wamtjela kutsi angakhatsateki ngaloko ngobe yena umane nje uyamsita ngobe amvela nekutsi vele yena kuyintfo yakhe kusita labanye bantfu labatihluphekelako. Onkhe emavi aDuduzile abebonakala atfola indzawo lenhle enhlitiyweni yaPhetsile futsi naPhetsile wavele watibonela kutsi lomuntfu lona umletselwe yinkhosi.

Duduzile wanela kubona kutsi Phetsile abetimisele mbamba ngemsebenti akabange angasachitsa sikhatsi watsi akahambe masinyane aye ekhaya ayolungisa timphahla takhe kute batophindze bahlangane ngaLwesihlanu weliviki lelitako khona lapha emakethe kaManzini bese uyamtsatsa kute aye naye eGoli. Noko, wamecwayisa ngekutsi kufanele angatjeli bantfu labanyenti ngaloku, ngobe yena akafuni kutsi ahlushwe bantfu labanyenti labatokuta kuye batomcela kutsi abasite ngemsebenti, ngobe naye abemane amsita ngobe amvela. Lesecwayiso sabonakala sinengcondvo kuPhetsile futsi watsi lendzaba utoyigcina phakatsi kwakhe naBabekati wakhe kuphela, ikakhulukati ngobe bekametsembisile nekutsi utomsita nangendzawo yekuhlala eGoli futsi amsite nekutsi angaphumela kanjani ngaphandle kwelive laseSwatini nanobe angenato tincwadzi tekuhamba.

Nembala wefika Lwesihlanu longali, Phetsile wavuka ekuseni walungiselela kuhamba ayohlangana naDuduzile emakethe kaManzini. Wavalelisa kuBabekati wakhe njengobe asalungela kuhamba, tavele tatehlela tinyembeti njengobe asavalelisa kuBabekati wakhe labemkhonte kakhulu katsi nakuye Babekati wakhe bese titehlela tinyembeti njengobe asacabanga kutsi nyalo bese kusikhatsi sekutsi ehlukane naPhetsile. Babekati wakhe wamcela kutsi njengobe abesati simo sekutihluphekela kwabo, abokhumbula ekhaya nangabe asacale kusebenta.

Nembala baphindze bahlangana boDuduzile naPhetsile ngaye Lwesihlanu khona emakethe kaManzini. Batsi kulindza kancane emotweni yaDuduzile njengobe Duduzile watsi kukhona umuntfu lamlindzele lovela eMaputo netimphahla takhe, labebavumelene ngekutsi batohlangana naye khona lapho emakethe kaManzini. Abalindzanga sikhatsi lesidze kwabe sekuchamuka intfombatana labeyitfwele tikhwama letimbili, yacondza ngco emotweni yaDuduzile lapho bebahleti khona naPhetsile. Watsi Duduzile angayibona wase uyaphuma emotweni kute ayihlangabete, naPhetsile wavele watibonela kutsi lona nguye lomuntfu labebamlindzele lobuya eMaputo netimphahla taDuduzile. Batsi kukhuluma kancane ngaphandle kwemoto boDuduzile nalentfombatana wase ukhipha imali uyayiniketa, wabe asatsatsa tikhwama letimbili watifaka emotweni, kwase kuba kwehlukana kwakhe nayo.

Bashaya bachitsa boDuduzile naPhetsile ngemoto baphikelela egedeni lelehlukanisa live laseSwatini nelaseNingizimu Afrika. Ngaphambi kwekutsi bafike emnceleni lowehlukanisa laseSwatini naseNingizimu Afrika, baphambukela esitolo lesiseceleni kwendlela base bayema lapho.

Duduzile watjela Phetsile kutsi kukhona bantfu labatobalindzela kulesitolo labebavumelene kutsi batohlangana lapho kute babasite ngekutsi Phetsile akwati kwewelela eNingizimu Afrika nobe angenato tincwadzi.

Batsi kulindza sikhashana lapho esitolo, base bayafika bafana lababili labebatosita Phetsile kutsi akwati kweca umncele waseSwatini ayongena eNingizimu Afrika nanobe angenato tincwadzi tekungena eNingizimu Afrika. Labafana bebatohamba naye ngetinyawo bayemecisa umcele lowehlukanisa live laseSwatini naseNingizimu Afrika bese bayohlangana naDuduzile ngale kulaseNingizimu Afrika. Ngaphambi kwekutsi batsatse Phetsile bahambe naye, Duduzile wabaniketa letikhwama takhe letimbili labebatiniketwe yintfombatana lebuya eMaputo watsi abahambe nato bayofohla nato emceleni ngetinyawo. Base bayehlukana, Duduzile wahamba ngemoto wayongena egedeni laseSwatini leliwelela eNingizimu Afrika kute ayobalindzela ngale ngaseNingizimu Afrika nangabe bona sebafohlile emceleni.

Nambala bafana bahamba naye Phetsile bate bamecisa umncele waseSwatini bangena eNingizimu Afrika, batfwele netikhwama letimbili taDuduzile labetiniketwe yintfombatana labeyivela eMaputo. Batfola Duduzile asabalindzele eceleni kwemgwaco lomkhulu lowendlula egedeni lasemnceleni lowehlukanisa laseNingizimu Afrika kanye nelaseSwatini. Watsi Duduzile abasheshe bafake timphahla emotweni bese Phetsile agibele ngekushesha emotweni kute bahambe masinyane. Ngaphambi kwekutsi bahambe wabonga ngemsebenti labesewentiwe ngulabafana lababili wase ubaniketa imali yekubakhokhela ngemsebenti labamentele wona, wabatisa kutsi utophindze abatsintse ngalelinye lilanga nangabe asadzinga kutsi bamentele lomunye umsebenti.

Bashaya bacitsa boDuduzile kanye naPhetsile baphikelela khona kaMagabangejubane bate bayongena emtini waDuduzile loseKrugersdorp. Ngesikhatsi Phetsile efika emtini waDuduzile loseKrugersdorp kwaba sengatsi kuvuleka likhasi lelisha emphilweni yakhe futsi kwaba sengatsi ngukhona acala ngca kumati Duduzile kutsi bekangumuntfu lonjani. Watfola kutsi bekunalamanye emantfombatana lamabili labehlala khona emtini waDuduzile loseKrugersdorp labesamati kahle Duduzile kanye nemisebenti yakhe kutsi unjani. Lamantfombatana wona abebuya eZimbabwe, eta kuleli laseNingizimu Afrika aletfwa nguye Duduzile ngobe atsi utowasita ngemsebenti. Nawo njengaPhetsile wawangenisa kuleli laseNingizimu Afrika angenato tincwadzi tehamba letiwavumela kutsi angena kuleli.

Nanobe lamantfombatana lamabili labevele eZimbabwe abesambonile Duduzile kutsi ungumuntfu loshushumbisa bantfu netidzakamiva, kodvwa besekungekho langakwenta ngobe abesavele atifakile enkingeni. Kantsi nawo bekasabonga kutsi ayakwati kuphila ngaloko lokuncane labe awayenga ngako atsi uyawaholela ngemsebenti webumnyama labementela wona.

Phela lelikhaya laDuduzile belinendzawo lesasitolo lesincane lapho lamantfombatana bekatsengisa khona tintfo letimbalwa emini kute emaphoyisa anganaki kakhulu nangabe abona bantfu bangena futsi baphuma emtini wakhe. Loku bekwenta emaphoyisa nobe abona bantfu kodvwa acabange kutsi bantfu labete kutotsenga. Kantsi kusihlwa abetsi utsengisa kudla lokulula khona lapho kuleso sitodlwana sakhe.

Loko labekwenta bantfu nakusihlwa bahlale baphuma bangena emtini wakhe. Labanyenti babo bebetela kutotsenga tidzakamiva. Bekutsi ngalesihlanu atsatse imoto yakhe ahambe nalamantfombatana kute ayowabeka etindzaweni letiphitsitela bantfu eceleni kwemahhotela endzawo kute atsengise ngemitimba bese awalandza ekuseni.

NaPhetsile wagcina asabonile kutsi nakuletikhwama letimbili labebatiletselwe yintfombatana lesuka eMaputo ngesikhatsi besuka eSwatini betigcwele tona tidzakamiva. Nanobe kwacale kwabamatima ngaPhetsile kwenta lomsebenti webumnyama labewentiwa nguDuduzile kodvwa bekatsi nangabe amkhumbuta ngematfuba lamanyenti emsebenti labemetsembise wona, avele abhoke ngelulaka Duduzile atsi ngumuphi umsebenti lawufunako ngobe umsebenti ngulona lamniketa wona.

In The Middle

by Lendyll Naicker

We'd enrolled. Little men in moustaches being suave around women that knew we were geeks. High school. Facial hair at thirteen. It was juvenile. Our hair grew quick and fast. Even in Africa (thought it had been the climate, India being near the equator and that. but it's not. we're hairy anywhere – Africa included. I've made peace with that). I am Segren Maharaj. I am twenty five years old. My name's a paradox. Segren is Tamil and Maharaj is Hindi. Back in the old country Hindi people would not marry Tamil people – who were of a lower caste. But we aren't in India now. I am South African. There is no caste system here. A bearded Hindi man married a Tamil woman and made me. I live in an Indian township. Hate calling it that. It's in between. We have shops and malls and homes and shacks and poverty. Money, too. All in one. There is a lot of crime. And drugs. Gangsters sell sugars. Not the sweet kind. Rat poison and crack mixed together. Brutal. And clever students score good grades and escape to white neighbourhoods. They change their accents and everything. I didn't get good grades. My teacher's tried to beat them out of me. They try to beat something out everyone. Today still. Smoking – bang. Fancy hair – bang. Holding hands – bang bang. But I read a lot. It's how I escape to white neighbourhoods. I did good at the lower grades. Primary school. My ma used to wake at the crack of dawn and make roti, which is cheaper than bread. Flour and water and a pinch of salt on a hot thava – that's frying pan in some Indian language. The fillings were moderate. Butter and jam or dhal curry. She used to roll them up – rotirolls. An Indian hot dog on a budget. Apartheid had just ended and I had no idea. History class changed though. We stopped learning about Wolraad Woltemade (a Dutchman that rescued Cape Town sailors from drowning) and found out who Nelson Mandela and the ANC were. And Tokyo Sexwale – Pronounced See-qwa-le. The poor veteran. He's a fat kid - he's a sex whale. Sex whale sex whale sex whale. Bang. We learned a new national anthem. And songs in Zulu. We were to round our mouths and click our tongues. Nkosi Sikelel' iAfrika. Lord Bless Africa. Click click. We didn't know what sex was but wanted to have it. I want to do sex with Miss V Singh. I scribbled that on a concrete wall the once. They announced it at assembly - the culprit wasn't fingered, thank God. She was pretty in her coloured saris. Like a peacock. One saying Namaste. A Hindi peacock! She taught math and physical education. And didn't hit us. She was sexy. I was the best at math. She injured her middle finger during netball one time. Had it placed in a cast. When she wrote (9 x 9 =?) it looked as if she was flipping the bird. We'd raise our middle fingers up to her behind and giggle. Up yours too, mam. Eighty-one mam. I'm sure she knew. Some of us had Christian names. Some of us were Christian. David. John. Garret. Eating rotirolls. Even a Christian named Christian. What's your name? Christian. No, not your religion! Ha Ha! I had the one grey pants that were washed every Friday and dusty black shoes with a hole at the left big toe. No-one laughed. Everyone had a hole somewhere. Sometimes someone would walk in crying before class. It meant that his/her mum had been beaten and he/she was sad. No one said anything. Not even the teachers. You can't know. Sweep it under the rug then. We'd have a cultural day every once a year. Which was useless given we were all Indian. Fun though. I remember wearing a white kurta and dancing to a song made famous by a Tamil sex whale from Durban. I screwed the light bulb and gyrated my hips. I mouthed the words: My wife saw me talking to another girl; and she said naa ne poi te vaa re! Others joined in. Everyone laughed. I still don't know what it means. I have no siblings. I brushed my teeth with coal when there was no toothpaste. My ma would grate it into a saucer and smear it onto a miniature blue toothbrush. It made my teeth white. I had bad breath. I avoided girls. They were stupid. Not Kajal. She had a gold nose ring. It was polished, shiny. Her parents told the principle it was religious. They were part of the governing body. They must not have hit her. And she liked pizza and captain planet. There were about fifty of us to a class. The jargon started at grade six. Hello – Watkind. How are you? – How's it vying? I'm luka ekse – I'm good. We learned from brothers and sisters. People with money were larney's. On it spun. Cool geeks. Luka. I gave her a pretty card on the final day. With a drawing of Captain Planet. I traced it. And a fifty cent coin glued to the inside. Thought it was pure gold. And made it known. You are more precious than gold, from Segren. I ran. She went to a different high school. I ran. Things changed. We changed. Vodka. Brandy. Women. Bra straps. Hitting. Stealing. Needles. Pipes. Sugars. But that's a different story. I stopped. I want to go back. I'd like to finish. That's how it vies. Bang.

FIVE HAIKU
by Abigail George

Ouma

Raging against life –
On this crooning sleeping planet;
She has fierce pride.

Oupa

This man in my blood,
history – this man is a son;
He feels deprived.

What does love mean then?

When that terrible
Scar is gone – far flung, sealed,
The art is not to fail.

For something that time forgot

No one knows my secrets.
I'm keeping it that way –
For selfish reasons.

The sofa

It is almost angelic, snug –
The way this light transforms
Hunched shoulders.

jamming

by Zama Madinana

in shosholoza
we jam
in a dam
of alcohol
but where is a condom
in this night
of drunken ladies

saliva escapes from
the bars of our lips
as they expose their assets

should we risk our lives
in this rain
of uncertainty

but lets keep on jamming
the night is still toddling
and the dj is still killing it

THREE POEMS
by Ahimsa Timoteo Bodhran

Du Bois before Accra

Talented Tibetan Tenth. Traveler. Who in your family doesn't have a degree?

The places you feel comfortable in are the places my family built and cleaned.
You have not worked before, are unfamiliar with what it means to have a job.

Your family didn't want to spoil your education.

My hands known floors, dishes, pots and pans, the cleaning of kennels, stretch
of garbage latex against skin, lick me with that, wooden splinters of mops, badge
of security, smell of dogshit and urine, bleach.

Perhaps you will see homelands I have never known.
Perhaps you will receive passport stamps from them in languages I cannot read.

rough

we sniff salts to move us back into consciousness.
give me the recipe for ammonium carbonate.
too rough, you said, in my hands,
even in bed too eager, left you sore where you didn't want to be.
this baby born without lotion.
yours was a high class mixing.
mine, ghettos y barrios, people who'd never flown in a plane,
only knew this land. yours, a diplomat's diaspora.
tus padres: modelos. your six languages? lose count, stumble with my few.
i trade you mango-wet kisses by the projects.
roaches scatter.
you see the world laid out wide before you.
i see stones in the path, am checked for weapons at the gate.
you float on through, emptied oysters at your lips,
pearls and abalone around your neck.
my soon-to-be-revoked passport.
you are always arriving, and i always waiting for departure.
comment on my way of eating,
my inarticulate manner of speech.
you shift red to my blue at this station, Doppler effect.
hurtle life. i am surprised our trains do not collide.

In the warm of the gallery space

I fail to see the beauty
of brown skin
on concrete.

this street you have kept warm. the store entrance
you have made your home for the night.

Perhaps I am not
an artist
of the people,
only someone
too close
to care.

misting between the tiles, we emerge
from our joint shower, explore
reassure with touch.

Cropped in, still stills,

one day disappear, not see you again.

right angles and tax refunds,

i visit the places in which i knew you,

so little to spare

hold your poems and letters for safe-keeping
watch for your name in periodicals

if only a nickel
and dime

check the web from time to time, keep your memory

alive.

could do it.

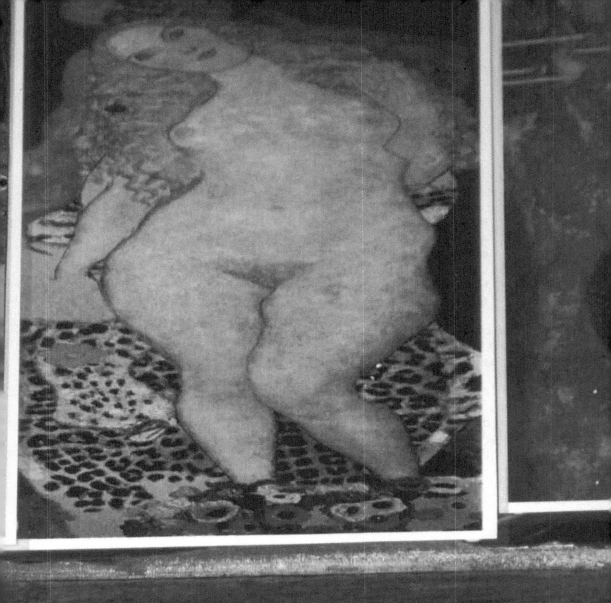

RIGHT OF ADMISSION
RESERVED

Backyard Mechanic
by Andre van Vuuren

sy kortbroekie span styf oor sy boude as hy
sy kop en skouers laat wegraak in die donker
dieptes van my kewer en hy, met ghriesbesmeerde vingers,
dit probeer ongedaan maak wat die tyd verweer het

'n rokershoes laat hom sy kop vinnig lig
en kug hy aamborstig agter 'n breë werkershand
"die skade is nie te erg nie," hyg hy uitasem,
"dit sal jou net 'n sixpack kos"

sy kundigheid gee vleuels aan my voete
terwyl syne doelloos rondskuif in die sand

Psalm of a Parliamentarian
by Piet Rampai

The state is my Shepherd, I shall not want;
It makes me to lie down in a subsidized house
It leads me into political tranquility;
It restores my faith in a lucrative future.
It leads me into paths of BEE and pensions,
For its international reputation's sake
Even though I walk through the valley
Of the shadow of corruption
I will fear no scorpions
For the state is with me, its police and troops
Comfort me.
It preserves for me a bank account, in the presence
Of devaluation.
It fills my pockets with allowances, my salary
Overflows.
Surely increments and promotion shall follow
Me, all the days of my life
And I shall dwell in senior staff quarters forever.
Viva.

The Interview

by Deon-Simphiwe Skade

As we walk silently down a large corridor leading to the regional manager's office, I realize that Palesa, the Human Resources consultant escorting me there, is something to behold. Not only does she have a personable face, but also an admirable physique. It's the body type that would not escape an indulging male eye.

She may not be aware of it, but hell, her confident and almost calculated strides are the very reason why I cannot avoid looking at her rear. She has full buttocks that are well defined, firm. And her steps, perhaps deliberately exaggerated to achieve something pleasing, seem to embellish her appearance. She walks in confident swings that have a nonchalant aspect about them, but graceful enough to appeal. Those swings, as I watch earnestly, open up an avenue in me that leads to an awkward form of ambivalence. I find myself caught between two feelings: admiration and lust. And both these feelings, as different as they may be to each other, possess almost equal power. But because of the way each half of Palesa's rear moves, rhythmic, forceful, my eyes enticed by lust. Each step from her long legs reveals the volume of the flesh covering either half of her bottom. The beige pants concealing the skin of her lower body, cling on to her as if for dear life. And as if she has somehow sensed the attention I have so fully given to the part of her body, she walks briskly. This only increases the pounding sound her stiletto heels make when they connect with the shiny floor. And all the while I watch with great interest at how each half of her rear moves about as if thrown around with carelessness known so intimately. The display is captivating, perhaps detrimental too for a married man of my calibre. I should not look so earnestly at things that may lead to my fall.

As I pay more attention to Palesa's walk, the squawking sound of her heels reminds me of the reason I'm there in the first place – the interview for the position of a junior shipping manager I applied for. But sadly, this recollection does little to keep my mind off the swinging beauty before me. I fail to even go through the mental notes that I made earlier in preparation for the interview. These notes I would have to remember in order to remain calm while seating in front of a stranger that would be conducting the interview. One has to be thoroughly prepared for such things. Otherwise lack of preparation cannot be concealed; it shows badly. Even the smallest obstacle may unsettle one in an interview; and as a result may cost one the only chance of getting into a job. One has to be articulate. Confident articulation seals the deal.

"Kwaak kwaak, kwaak" the pounding of Palesa's shoes is relentless. Her swings on the other hand, seem to be mocking me. It's like they are saying: 'look, but do so at your own peril; you may be swung into darkness.' But my eyes remain stubborn.

Despite the sound of the shoes, there's silence. But its presence is brief, only falling between Palesa's steps.

"It's here!" Palesa says as we reach the last door of the corridor, ending my private treat instantly. "I'm going to leave you with Sharon, Mr. Oosthuizen's secretary. Maybe I'll see you again after your interview."

I nod. Palesa then opens the door with the same vigour she had put into her walk, leading me into the office. I manage to read the sign on the door before it closes: Operations Suite it says. Inside, a young lady with an office face greets us cheerfully. I notice her insincere grin that flashes as fast as the silence that fell in the hallway. I have seen that kind of a smile far too often to notice one immediately.

"Hey Sharon, here's Mr Mokoena. He has a ten o'clock with Mr Oosthuizen."

"Absolutely! Mr Oosthuizen has been expecting him. He's just busy on the line right now, but he'll be done soon," replies Sharon, stretching out her hand for a handshake.

"Good morning Mr. Mokoena! Welcome."

My big, strong hand swallows Sharon's tiny one with ease. I feel a little awkward but manage a coy smile to which she reciprocates with a flash grin she passes as a smile.

"Would you like me to get you some coffee or tea while you wait Sir?" Sharon's tone is the most polite one I've ever heard. It's all years of business etiquette.

"No, thank you! I had some coffee earlier," I reply, hoping to equal her zealous politeness.

She turns to Palesa and say: "Well I suppose you have already given Mr Mokoena the job placement forms to fill in."

"Yes, I have. But I'll double check just in case we missed something."

The two ladies then lower their voices. I suspect their talk to be non-work-related, for their faces lose the professional aura they both displayed through their faces and speech. Perhaps they are talking about what to eat for lunch. All the while I struggle to scrutinize Palesa's body because Sharon is there; she occasionally casts her eyes at me as if to warn me not to look at the source of my lust, which until this point I still refuse to acknowledge wholly. I kiss what would have been my last treat on Palesa goodbye.

"Okay then," says Palesa finally, increasing her voice and turning to me. "I guess I'll see you later Mr. Mokoena."

I look at her eyes. They are a brown pair that has delicateness that seems to be hiding malice that may light up at the slightest provocation. But they also have an admirable determination I find difficult to overlook. And before I know it I'm taken by the ambiguous light that may bring glee and frown all the same. And for some reason, perhaps overcome by such bewitching pair of eyes, I allow this moment to linger on.

In all my wishes of this morning, the success of the interview ahead having taken a backseat, I find myself wishing to know Palesa a little more. She's a beautiful girl with an equally appealing body shape.

"Mr. Mokoena! Did you perhaps hear what I said?" asks Palesa, slightly bewildered.

"Indeed. I'll come to your desk after the interview Palesa."

"Okay then, I'll see you later," she leaves with the same vitality I admire very much now. As expected, I don't catch the last glimpse of her rear – Sharon is like a hawk.

"May I use the bathroom please?" I cease the opportunity so that I can go and do the last preparation before the interview.

"Of course! You'll find the men's one three doors down the hallway." Her clumsy smile comes and goes as fast.

"Thank you!"

I leave the Operations Suite and walk down the hallway. I count three doors. At the third door, a large sign hangs above: Toilet, it says. A naughty smile reaches my lips. I know I should have noticed the damn sign earlier. Nonetheless, I walk into the toilet to do the type of business toilets are made for. My presence is short though; it's for a quick release of water that may cause me any discomfort during the interview. I wash my hands and leave.

On my way back to the Operations Suite there's silence that occasionally rises between my steps. Somehow this silence seems more noticeable than my footsteps. It seems to hum obstinately, interrupted only by my relaxed steps. For a short while I think about Palesa. Now I long to see her walk one more time, those swings! But a mild regret gets ignited, fluffs desperately until it becomes a strong force. But I suppress it. I mean I know it's not fair on my wife. But then who can resist Palesa's allure? I decide to put such conflicts aside. I need to be ready for the interview. I have to be sharp.

*

Mr. Oosthuizen means to harm me with his steely-blue stare as I talk about my background. He looks cold, somewhat cynical. And his attempts to conceal such profound expression by masking it with a frail veiled cordial face, falls flat on the table like a startling revelation. Maybe it's my accent he doesn't like; or my gestures as I articulate some ideas. All the potential harm he could unleash is restrained by the solemnity of the interview he allows to overwhelm me, the silence around me as I talk. He can turn things around. He has that kind of look that could break a man. If it's not wounding my ego that he achieves, then I'm certain he'll ensure that he strips off any shred of confidence in me. Then I'll be as good as not being in this sullen room trying to talk my way into a job.

I may not present myself well. My thoughts may be incoherent. Obtrusive looks do that to me sometimes. On the other hand, if I yield to this pressure, Mr. Oosthuizen would be victorious. I can see him gloating at the end of it all, perhaps pleased with his underhand tactics that no one would dare question. I mean no one! There are no rules against such things, meanness and all these unspoken attacks. He knows that he would not be asked to explain why I did not make it in the record for the shortlisted candidates. The least his fellow seniors may ask him, if they'd bother, could be whom he thought made a better candidate out of all those he'd seen. With the way things are going, I may not feature in that talk about the most suitable candidates. Even if I were to complain about Mr. Oosthuizen and his bad tactics after the interview, no one would believe me. He's a damn Regional Manager of a big warehousing firm for crying out loud.

"Have you worked in a warehouse environment before?" asks Mr. Oosthuizen with a bladed tone, his eyes steady with malice.

A feeling of resentment spurs up in me, fierce like a terrible heart burn. I want to curse him, to tell him that his look may wound me badly and cost me a job. That he's not nice at all. That I know that his motives are bad – but his question about my experience prevents me from doing so – it demands an immediate answer.

An entry in my CV spells out my tangible work experience – I worked in a warehouse environment for at least three years. It's there! Maybe he means to discredit my claim.

"Yes Sir, I have," I respond. "In fact I fulfilled various functions within the same warehouse."

He tilts his head a little, so that his eyes may shine from the glow of the light that watches passively over the proceedings. His thin lips bend into an awkward twist like he's annoyed by my short answer, while his eyes menacingly lock their stare forever into me without blinking. He seems to be using every trick at his disposal to unsettle me, before his skeptical lips could throw out another question at me.

"Well, Mr. Mokoena; tell me about these 'functions' you performed as you put it," he requests with a tone that casts doubt on my choice of words by emphasizing the word 'functions' in his question.

For a moment I think about the definition of the word itself. Function. F.U.N.C.T.I.O.N. It's obviously a noun; a verb also. And in my response it served as a noun. I don't have any uncertainties about that part. It's true! I fulfilled roles that would have otherwise been performed by persons with relevant job titles. Yet I was not officially appointed to fulfill those roles. I was just a mere Picker as my pay-slip reflected. Not a Dispatch Supervisor or any of the many roles I performed. My official title demanded of me to pick stock and distribute it within the warehouse accordingly.

"Sir, I acted as a Dispatch Clerk, a Stock Controller, a Receiving Clerk and a Shipping Team Supervisor," I say, assuming a more cautionary mode of talking, seeing that the prevailing circumstances demand such of me. Bladed eyes remain quiet.

I suddenly feel a great sense of relief not because Mr. Oosthuizen collapsed his sharp stare back into my CV and repositions himself in his chair after my response. In fact, I feel triumphant, more so for responding correctly to his question without contradicting the actual truth about my warehouse experience – I fulfilled roles, but it did not end there. I earned enormous experience that would work in my favour in many similar future job applications.

Mr. Oosthuizen then looks into my CV for a long time, and slowly, his lips straighten giving him a friendly look. "Well, you seem to have done a lot in your three years there – I'm impressed!" he says. "Now, tell me about yourself; your strengths and weaknesses. You may also tell me about your interest outside the formal working environment."

His face becomes warm like that of a concerned parent. A sudden rush of confidence wells up chest quelling my wound. I feel it scurry and permeate throughout my body reviving my optimism. Something suggests that I may get the job after all. But I also I fear the effect I may leave on Mr. Oosthuizen after talking about my strengths and weaknesses, my private thoughts. I get too honest and personal with these things it's impossible for anyone not to be moved. I had left a few people in emotive state when it got to this part of the interview. I become very candid, even going as far as talking about my wife whom I love dearly. And knowing that recruiting persons have a soft spot for married individuals due to their perceived sense of reliance and focus, I usually make a meal of it. I philosophize about the whole thing and drive the interview to a whole new frontier. And when I reach that part, I get an assurance from my gut that I may definitely get the job. I speak so thoughtful; I end up absorbing the interviewer into my interesting but uneventful life. All this I do when I speak about my life outside the work environment. Perhaps Mr. Oosthuizen may handle it like a man when such effect takes over him. He looked very tough earlier on. I'm sure he'd be alright. And maybe he'll hire me. And this will only exposed more to Palesa. I wonder what Mr. Oosthuizen thinks of her. I wonder if he has seen how she pounds the floor with those stilettos and how that bottom swings when she walks. Maybe like me, and perhaps with fear of anyone finding out, Mr. Smith indulges his eyes without anyone knowing. He has a sharp eye that would not miss such a spectacle as Palesa's rear.

*

Sharon walks me back to the main reception area after the interview. We find Palesa seated behind her desk engrossed in some document.

"Here's Mr. Mokoena. Goodbye Sir!" says Sharon with that smile of hers.

"Thank you Sharon! I'll wrap up now."

"I'm sure all went well with the interview," Palesa says handing me a form. "You did not fill in the top part. There you go."

The area in question is the one that requires my ID number and some personal details. It's about four lines. I fill the form in and hand it back to Palesa. I take the opportunity availed by our solitude to pursue a personal matter.

"Um, I don't mean to be rude or anything like that. I wish to give you a compliment," I say deepening my voice so that I may be taken seriously.

"Of course, Mr Mokoena; I'm listening."

"Well, you look beautiful. Is it any way possible to have coffee with you some day?"

"Oh, that? I never notice much of how I look. But thank you for the kind words! But I'm afraid we should keep things professional, shall we?"

I nod reluctantly, a wave of embarrassment sweeps over my face but I keep a polite and proud appearance despite the rejection. I should not worry much about it; I have my wife. But deep inside I'm wounded and this Palesa should not see. The excitement over how well the interview went also dies immediately.

Soiled Sheeeeeeetsssssss ah!!
by Pamella Dlungwana

salt in grab a crotch...
not much here to hold on to
seconds into forever...
somesilentacknowledgemento
fonenightstand

tents for homes
plastic jug mug/sho'ttttttt
kwerekwere Go Home!! Sssssssstop!!
nobrotherhereonmygoodwillafricandiasporafuckkkk'd

mic stand/check
media smile UNapology
sister squeamish pushed into bracken (brackets?) Sprag/ken
how did the Germans term it?

taxi shuffle
slow mumbles
new identities/Lenin/Amin/Taylor/Muga (be?)

midnight trysts with diabolical angels
with memos on how to fan this flame one wing at a time
lie undocumented at the feet of ambitious boabablings

saltingrabacrotch...
scratch that itch

For Unto Us a Child is Born

by Dick Mafuba

I wrung the towel with my weak hands. The red blood flowed into the bucket. The whole floor was soaked. My whole body went livid with the heat, and the heavy pain felt like molten lead was being poured over the top of my head. And besides, the painful cramps in my stomach signaled the impending offset of yet another withdrawal sickness.

I wiped my weak, watery eyes and blew my running nose into the wet towel. I forced my weak muscles to move and sat in a corner. I took off the wet t-shirt and hugged my aching legs. My whole body felt itchy and irritable....

There was a knock on the door. I forced my heavy eyelids to open. It was a while before I could force my lips to move though:

"Whae is it?" I asked.

"Dee!"

"Jess aye minute," I replied.

It was struggle getting up. My whole body shook, and the effort sent shock waves of pain rushing down my spine. My head suddenly went numb and dizzy; I almost fell. I had to grab a hold of the door handle just to keep myself upright. I turned the key in the lock.

"Where did all this blood come from?" He asked, sternly. He was heating the contents of the spoon over that candle, which lit up the room like a Star of David shining upon an earie nativity scene. The way I was feeling I just couldn't waste any words on the homosexual. I just pointed at the plastic bag and the skinny, frail body curled like a feotus beneath the blood soaked bedspread.

The room was quiet, except for Faith's faint sobbing.

"Whose was it?" he asked, all of sudden now full of concern. I shrugged my shoulders. My whole mind was focused on what I was doing. I had wrapped the tie around my arm. My breadth was coming in short, sharp gasps and my hands were trembling. I had to wrap my arm around Dee who finally pierced the flesh and injected the needle slowly into the popped up vein. The stream of red blood flowed and filled the barrel of the syringe. Finally, I loosened the tie. ...

I had lit up a joint. Faith had finally stopped sobbing and fallen asleep over a crossword puzzle. I was telling Dee about the previous night:

"Christmas party. At her parents. 'For unto us a child is born' and all that jazz. Faith comes tae me n said: 'Emmanuel, don't drink. You know how you get after you've been drinking. I don't want any trouble tonight.'

Telt her ah didnae ken whit the fark she wis talking aboot.

So Ah down two boatels aye bevvys.

Dance.

Ah down a couple aye bevvys

Mingle.

Ah down a couple aye bevvys.

Chat. Ah'm chatting tae her blond-heided sister from London, likesay. Sais tae us:

'Emmanuel, I just love the way you talk. You've got a funny accent!'

'Aw aye! That's funny. Yuv goat a funny accent too!'

Cunt goes.

'I don't have an accent. You have.'

Ndikati.

'Sistah! Mune ark-sarnt.'

Cunt goes.

'No. I don't have an accent. You do.'

Ndikati.

Listen, bitch!

Jess coz Ah downt speak naw Angaise wid naw bloody Breeteesh accent dawnt farkin mean dat Ah goats two 'ave naw farkin accent so fark off, BITCH!'

Hand goes tae her mouth, bitch goes 'Aaaaargh!' Goes farkin red in the bloody face, n then she farks off!"

Dee had already unbuckled my pants. He was fondling me and continued to fuel my rod with his wet lips. I took a drag on the joint, and continued:

"Ah down two boatels aye bevy.

Hang around.

Ah down two boatels aye bevy.

Danced again.

Ah down two more boatels aye bevy.

Then it all began.

Ah slap Faith hard. Bitch starts greeting hysterically. Ah sais tae her.

'See what you made me do?'

Ah punch it in the face. Bitch gets a blue eye.

'See what you made me do?'

Ah punches it in the farkin mooth. Bitch screams. Bloods running down her dress. Ah sais tae her.

'Its your own farkin fault! See what you made me do?'

Ah boots it in the farkin stomach.

'SEE WHAT YOU MADE ME DO? BITCH! Keep your England and let me keep my Zimbabwe. WORSE THAN DOGS AND PIGS! This is Z-I-M-B-A-B-W-E! Why don't you go back to your own country?'"

Dee had stopped suddenly. Faith had woken up and was looking at us with a puzzled expression in her blue eyes.

"Will she be okay?" he asked.

"She'll be fine," I groaned, as I drew his head down , tossed my head backwards, and exploded into the roof of his mouth.

Three poems
by Hayly Chewins

we lie in bed somewhere warm and safe you tell me

we lie in bed somewhere warm and safe you tell me
things that make my heart ring
like a bell i always want you
soft strong beautiful you with eyes like the dark
part of the sun and skin like earth i pull my self
onto you and kiss your mouth your neck
your chest your hands are always a little rough and i love it
because you're gentle and you bite your lip and suddenly
you're every thing that ever existed
and i'm all that ever was

you're sleeping but i'm talking to you
nevertheless playing some game asking you where
you'd like to be kissed your eyes are shut but
your face is open your smile is creeping up into
your cheeks trying to be surreptitious and i am
in love with you so full bursting with that
love every cell in my body is going to explode at any moment
now any moment now i am going to cease to
exist with all the power that resides within me becoming
far far too much like a desert flooded you are just wordless

you're cutting apart chicken hot

you're cutting apart chicken hot
by the oven i don't know
where these fights emerge from break
through like scissors through cooked
skin there really isn't any thing
to argue about i feel
that frustrating warmth that can't be cooled by
any amount of water of dancing or sighs
arise it's pushing up my throat like
an apple bobbing in water leaking out
flooding in when you need me i can't be there
and when i need you like i always do
you're never around

i brought you coffee one morning

i brought you coffee one morning
(drove to fetch it from a fresh-smelling place)
i think i wanted our lives to be clean
like that morning
bite in the air

you stood hunched at the door
the aspirin on your breath
acrid and rotting

you threw the liquid down the back of your throat
and cursed its burn on your tongue

TWO POEMS
by Rosamund Handler

Psychiatric emergency

Boredom smells damp
the floor rises to her tongue
sits there   a throbbing molar
she's grateful for the pain
the waiting room no oasis
the grey walls won't engage
the vinyl chair cracked from agitated bums
agitates hers
morsels of the day
pincered by sunlight
skim lino floors
scabbed by tooth and nail
and the empty eyes of
those who have seen
green grass recently
now fast fading to black
to zero tolerance
for being where
the ceiling is glaze-eyed

where hands hang

lifeless things
even when a scream
drops into the thirsty air
lands in a smudge on the floor
like a secret she cannot divine
though she feels it wormy
beneath her inauthentic skin

she closes her eyes
feels her shoulder blades in
the palms of your hands
that ancient summer
when you and she and
dope and Jimi Hendrix
once exonerated yourselves

Man contemplates wife

Not too bad for sixty, is she?

mornings she liplessly
impales another suspect
cows the arrogant crinkle
in the weary mirror
snarl ironed by surgery
or another unguent
night-weathered brow
folded in creases
slack as hung laundry

scrutinizing her bum
she wails it's swelled overnight
like a cake in the oven
food her obsession
a beggar at all feasts
she dissects every bitter morsel
chews a disciplined few
reads the anguished dessert menu
drooling at lush women

who spoon up ice cream
while she skitters with yearning
every drip shivering down her gullet
gathering saliva and
raising goose bumps
from her fool's gold hair
to spiny bunions

from behind she's still
a yes no maybe
until she turns and bares
hands like broken kites
and freckled eyes
the prisons of her dying light

then she slips into
the nearest dessert menu
where she'll be gone
for at least a day

Emzana Shack Recollections
by L.SOJINI

Publisher: *Pole, Pole, Press (In association with Botsotso)*

Reviewed *by Mboneni Ike Muila*

1.1 emapozana shack recollections,
soos die pozana shack recollections,
is `n mnca reminder of a once was a mshengu wiel,
informal settlement pozana in my vicinity ekasi
in which all sort of people auties of
no particular origin converge for a hideout
oukies from broken homes en thieves
not forgetting people in dire need of a staan plek.
that is a place they could call home edladleni makoya
some are jail birds hardened criminals running away from the law
who escaped from a danyane, like springbok
not amabhokobhoko the national rugby team you know
bank robbers zolo stuff pusher marijwana soos mariwana that is ganja smokers
in other words..,others like wonke-wonke mbomboza skhambathi drinkers
in a small skhambazisa pozana of the drug lords en
the drug queens.., paddlers of all assorted mix masala you name it..,
that's more than just a state of anarchy
rampage emsawawa van mzansi
from zola mndeni emabhodini kam'shayazafe to jozi
vaya Soweto brazana van myne skuta chomie windsak zoomzananas emapozana rush
in zana current emoyeni tanakamina double slash njivana backup
support front opposite direction ek se..,
silaphanje.., emapozana shack recollections of kanjani..,
some fortunate enough people were relocated
to orange farm RDP houses en not so fortunate enough decided
to go to lahlu'mlenze joe slovo freedom park en
snake park informal settlement pozana to erect their shacks
all over around emsawawa mzansi van die rainbow nasie
en so aan the list is endless of amapozana shack erections without ground plan legality
or not, pozana recollection here pozana recollection there mushrooming en
emerging all over emzansi even in the heart
of the central business district
tot ook in my mental pozana as ek lees
die story van emapozana shack recollections
kom kry ek kan so maar ook visualize die prent
van die laatie-tjie wat slender is en ook
'n maer skinny lanky malankane van 'n laatie-tjie nogal..,
a slender youngster malankane soos die een voor enige grootman is ook 'n ntwana
just like when you addresses any younger kid that he is of his own age
amongst elders unlike a grootman wat in die tuin werk en addressed as
a garden boy by young once who claim to be his senior in terms of
the juleit under which he is hired en on the other hand mothers
who make tea for a company of younger male en females calls her a tea girl
en nou die laatie-tjie van `n ntwana, is as thin as a pin in such way that he is just..,

1.2   like a sticky manza-nza motsotsoropane van `n laatie-tjie
running as if his barefoot hardly touch the ground
he is not happy about his underfed body..,
the slender youngster malankane wishes to gain a few kilos en be stout as
in fatty boom-boom bhumba mapoempane with
a pot belly cooler box but not sluggish like those mgedezana so to say
die laatie-tjie youngster is van emapozana shack recollections by birth
die laatie-tjie ntwana van emapozana is nou gat vol with his underfed body
of which he says is like a hanger left on the wire hanging even those vups
he wears are not his choice en size kulondawo my bra en is not
the kind of hanging the slender youngster prefers.., emapozana shack recollections
is a clustered mapozana with shacks mkhukhus which appears as if
falling in their informal zigzag pathways without any proper town planner
on the ground settlement.., in fact emapozana shack recollections is a piece of land..,
a pozana that is unholy surrounded by kak en rubbish amagansa allover around
mix masala swampy kinder pozi which when sunrise heat intensifies it blesses
the whole of emapozana shack recollections by the unacceptable stench when
you analyze en there are no toilets facilities the only best toilet is the nearest bush
on the other hand the youngsters running is interrupted by the thought en the smell of
amagwinya from macanes spaza shop which his chomie mandilakhe warns the
youngster about macanes big fat oily gwinyas that she wipes her daughters bum en
without washing hands prepares gwinyas for the whole nation with all this woza-woza
tanakamina mkhozi uya khwezela kulondawo silaphanje..;
emapozana shack recollections with the zanas in no doubt uya bhaiza on the other hand
nogal, the slender youngster malankane is highly aware that most people
especially girls in the beauty contest en modeling could kill just to have a body like his
the one he so much wish to discard.., as long as the slender youngster malankane
masters his home language that is the mother tongue the one he owns from emapozana
like a musical instrument melody in unison mjojo grend grend moja tightly in tune
he can be in a position to command any other language without any qualms about it
cause i believe no one owns the English language in such a way that one could even
claim to be entered in guinnes records like the slender youngster malankane in character
remember all artist en creative writers including ordinary people from grassroots level
are creators of language en no qualms about all that ok.., right nothing to write home
about.., the slender youngsters ou matopana tamkhulu also advice malankane met lewe
omte se.., lewe is about relationship en getting along with any kind of people is what
he meant about relationship. ou-tamkhulu gives the youngster an example of..,
relationship yase spanini omte se, if he does not get along with chomies en mgedezana
it means he is having a sour relationship en that is part of life.., since then..,
the youngster uya denka very hard about the relationship.., ou Bess en Banda en die
hele van those mgedezana who always take their diski when they play diski down
the road.., he says hoe kan hy vergeet that mgedegede Sizos who should have been
a taima than a lazy student.., worst of all, young boys uya bavala en take their lunch
box en skut hulle sake vuil, en haal uit die hele pocket money die hele loose count
coins so as to afford himself a nkauza to smoke with his Buntu chomie sharing in the
toilets..,

1.3   during break time.., the youngster came to a verge of cutting esigele nokugeleza
in half to highlight a statement to those mgedezana that it takes effort tears en blood
to be present esigele, their school teachers find pleasure in beating them for sweet
nothing when they arrive late esigele or when they don't know the answer to
questions which they themselves could not answer at their varsity lectures, Sizo
en those mgedegede paint a picture of a bitter relationship, the slender youngsters ou..,
matopana tamkhulu also speaks of relationship gone sour.., while running along
the crooked pathway of emapozana shack recollections he accidentally..,
bumped into mgedezana ou madala drumming in his stomach with his right
shoulder en that's where he lost all the protection fee lozi which he was supposed
to pay the land lord king bra zakes of emapozana shack recollections ou madalas
hand held him by the collar of his tee shirt no chance of letting himself loose
availed he tightened his grip on his neck prohibiting the air that brought him
crashing into madala, everybody all the zanas flocked around to see the first hand action
in full view of those mgedegede ou madala dragged the slender youngster malankane
like a trash of can refusing to enter the trash truck at the same moment ou madala..,
accusing the slender youngster of mugging him instead of zanas helping the poor young
oukie out people of emapozana shack recollections cheered on when the youngster
was thrashed broad daylights off with his short ncaza stripped down exposing his yellow
mapunapuna ezi pepenene in public of emapozana who were for ever laughing the slender
youngster malankane crying out of embarrassment keeping his poorly underfed
body frame flat on the naked ground.., as a form of defence the youngster realized that
the whole tsunami was not just about him ou madala did not see eye to eye with his
grandfather ou tamkhulu they were like ghost, he once left en came back to find his beer
done finish en klaar only the lonely empty lay on the ground like a fallen king if he knew
that the beer would cause such a rift he could have took it along with him from that
day on ou tamkhulu had a grudge with madala, what ou madala did to the youngster
was a joy ride trip to hell en back before the crowd of emapozana shack recollections..,
every month all good emapozana shack dwellers the so called zanas cough up some rent
zaka which ou makhulu the youngsters grand oulady call it protection fee zaka a lozi
which got lost when the youngster bumped into madala ou magriza works hard indeed
for the rental fee lozi selling smoked russians fried fish sweets en loose draw cigarettes
at the market place in town in order to pay the land lord bra zakes illicit rental fee lozi
collection scheme if you skip your protection fee zaka he tosses his lunatic thugs Titus
en Nko his sons in the centre fold to come repossess your property.., ou makhulu also
cook chow food stuff for hungry hard working construction contract workers who pay
after the end of each month.., in order to regain the rental protection fee lozi he lost he
plotted to sellout Sviwe to Titus Zacharias son.., that the charmer pretty biza Svidge is
going around proclaiming that Zanele is carrying his bambino the youngster en his
chomie Mandilakhe collaborated in writing a letter to Titus son of the landlord bra
zakes about the two promiscuous Sviwe en Zanele.., mandilakhe het eits sensational
geskryf vir hom bras the slender youngster malankane so as to win Titus over en
recover the protection fee lozi he lost when he accidentally bumped into ou madala,
the youngster en hom chomie mandilakhe weet for a fact that hulle kan ou Titus
maklike con, Titus en Nko hulle is so maar lunatics who perceive themselves as the
princes of emapozana shack recollections..,

1.4 ou tamkhulu en the oulady magriza grand parents of the youngster decided to go on a vacation umakhulu ou magriza to the youngster left him in the hands of his auntie Mavis to safeguard her business while she is away auntie Mavis is from Ngangelizwe Mthatha miles away from emapozana en she wont be leaving sooner than the home coming of magriza she also want to pay a tribute to her bosom chomie who was like a sister to her, Zoleka who passed on about a month ago she could not attend her funeral en if she does not pay her last respect to Zoleka she feels en believe it would be a disgrace on her side.., on the morning the youngsters grandparents left auntie Mavis arrived emapozana shack recollections.., malankane en his chomie Mandilakhe assisted auntie Mavis in pushing the business trolley to the market en setting up the table auntie Mavis gave them her golden wrist watch so that they should come back to the market every half an hour to check if she still have enough change en water on their way back to emapozana they walked staggering like soldiers bruised by war the heat intensity cooking mix masala rubbish dispatching an intensified stench that blesses the whole of.., emapozana shack recollections all of sudden a autie drags them to a steel zinc shack.., the black robed jimbos.., u darkie the black Italiano – aka the sars man.., die autie is van lahlu'mlenze who calls emapozana emzet.., he claims to be a tax collector who knows his plans moves around with a dreadlocks beast of a man sporting a black vest recruiting youngsters to become a marijwana paddlers selling ganja to users en addicted smokers in zanana.., that is emapozana shack recollections en promises to leave a system that will.., generate a healthy zaka flow for themselves every day en every week the black Italiano gives the youngster Malankane the stuff en tells him that if he is a true hustler he will convert the ganja stuff into good zaka goeie lozi mnca mula en that he does not have to sell himself otherwise his mother will not see him again meaning he will end up a danyane in a cell, the slender youngster malankane was the last one to exit the steel zinc shack while walking home there was a van on his trail, the youngster stepped up his pace because he did not trust these guys they abduct you en strip your body parts for the so.., called ngoma lucky charm they make crappy deals which bring them enormous wealth at the expense of their family members life when you look around you see mutilated bodies dumped under the bridge how do you explain kids who are without their reproductive organs its all in the name of making dirty zaka that's why you see the slender youngster malankane running away from this van these guys spotted him while on his way out of that tin shack en now they are keeping an eye on him en so he had to duck for survival as his pace was beginning to crescendo the van caught up with him the man on a drivers seat beckoned the youngster in a berating manner to get inside the van just a few moment after he got his hands on the ganja stock while they were driving away with the youngster they say to malankane you listen to us ntwana en follow what we say to you accordingly not so we will throw you in a damn river with hungry monsters, the youngster said to them he bought the ganja stuff, he just wanted to smoke marijwana en is his first time he saw others doing it en thought it was cool en for that matter he is not addicted they also took the wrist watch of aunt Mavis from the youngster en ask him as to where did he steal the watch the youngster told them it was his aunties watch he did not steal it, they said he was planning to sell it en buy another round, he denied en they left the youngster by the roadside en told the youngster what is expected of him en that they are not after the..,

1.5 youngster, they are looking for syndicates behind these drug trafficking scoundrels en from now on he is officially their eye any mistake from his side they will track him down en he will spend the rest of his life in a dark cell that is a danyane.., the youngster had to walk back home from where they left him on his own through the dreary night.., on what transpired while the youngster was lost in a karoo his chomie Mandilakhe says he got that on good authority from the former bursaries officer but the youngster says he himself narrates everything as if he was there in person all in all these are his own tales remember the slender youngster malankane himself plotted all this twist en jive of zanas en soul sellout of Sviwe.., pretty biza Svidge who charms ladies like Zanele without zaka no mula to maintain the love relationship at hand en the coming bambino Malankane came with the idea of selling pretty biza Sviwe to Titus son of the landlord bra Zakes.., the youngster then collaborated with his chomie Mandilakhe to draft a letter which they then sent to Titus en Nko. the lunatics sons of the landlord king bra Zakes of all the zanas emapozana shack recollections.., in order to recover money that the youngster lost when he accidentally bumped into ou madala, indeed this is his recollections nobody else deserves glory in these pages.., the slender youngster malankane is the one en only ntwana amongst zanas who can be associated with the phrase.., every swane en poole glory en no one else not even a reader in these pages if it comes to glory period prince Titus the zanas lunatic demanded himself entry into the pretty biza Sviwes tjoks mkhukhu saying they don't want him they just want his ugly face Svidge was not willing to open up Titus suggested to his younger brother Nko. that they put paraffin all over his tjotjombe in that way he will know better not to mess up with the Nzuzos next time his thing itches.., pretty biza Svidge demanded to know what they want from him they demanded in return that he open up by force not so they will demolish the door open en chop his head off en return to their father with his gobhane on a silver tray.., he was left without any option en now fearing for his life pretty biza Sviwe finally opened up the mkhukhu door inside his tjoks Titus saw en identified his blanket which appeared like a skoroplaap before his eyes on top of Sviwes boat – look-alike bed en panties which Nko remembers putting their name tags on them including Titus rugby boot bhathu size thirteen.., another rugby bhathu boot fell blowing dust from the ground.., in the mist of the dust pretty biza Sviwe was severely slapped down on the dusty ground with a lightning take five labhabha heavily on the face like the rugby bhathu boot he had watched fall Titus obnoxiously loathed pretty biza Svidge for clipping the petals off his rose Zanele.

On the flip side Zanele never loved Titus he was ugly an a lunatic unable to read en he could not match her standards she only got into Titus relationship because Yandisa – yaras.., had been in a danyane emalangeni since Sviwe was not supporting her that is in terms of material goodies en party bills then Nko the younger Nzuzo proposed a fortnight timeline between Titus en the pretty biza Sviwe to go on a fiya go fiya fight street fist clash fiya go.., hai bamba hai luma in public with all the zanas around watching the two of them battle it out, between the two the one left standing takes the girl Zanele along with her package according to the youngster malankane the all knowing Narrator, a real woman with true love does not make it an issue that you have no zaka or that awu theshi haba thesho you don't have a juleit on the night the two guys left the slender youngster by the side of the road to walk his way home on his own feet, wa bhathuza dapper en stapper tot emapozana.

1.6 When auntie Mavis wanted her golden wrist watch back the slender youngster malankane told auntie Mavis emshayashaya nge two six nine nine that the golden wrist watch fell on the ground en then wa ganda over it ngempazamo but she need not worry because he took it for repairs en they promised he will get it back the next day, aunt Mavis was so sweet en nice grend moja to the youngster en she never harassed him for her golden wrist horlosie only to realize later that she was madly in love with the landlord king bra zakes, aunt Mavis uya jola is waar with the father of Titus en Nkosinathi the zanas lunatics en that alone was a biggest blunder his aunt have ever committed on the side of the slender youngster malankane in emapozana shack recollections every time mabhulu cries when not hungry sitting with half of a nzomela next to his pile of scraps, everyone knows something is about to take place en is about that fortnight timeline van fiya go fiya fight the street fist fight between Titus en the charmer pretty biza Svidge emapozana residents emerged from all corners, as the youngster in his own phrase would say.., every swane en poole gathered around most of them were knew faces appearing for the very first time at this fateful event en it seems as if the slender youngster malankane this is where he coined his phrase.., every swane and poole.., referring to the zanas of emapozana men en women his own fancy way no qualms about that, writings on the mapozana paper is like writings on the wall for everyone to see en digest then uzikhuphule mapozana way jy weet mos if at all ziyakhipha, the pre-match fight started between Nko. en Ngwatu ka Sijadu cause in every showdown hosted by the Nzuzos you don't just bring your eyes you pay for the showdown the youngster realized that his ghost ou madala was there too en already paid his showdown fee lozi en happy that he is going to see the warm up pre-match fight mahala.., rebellious Ngwatu ka Sijadu refused to pay for the showdown to Nko. who was collecting en demanding the showdown fee zaka with his whip in a hand, Ngwatu was in control of the fight en almost defeated the young.., nzuzos spoiled brat prince Nko. who was down en out with his own whip. Ngwatu was distracted by bra zakes the landlord king in the crowd into abandoning the fight, Nko. picked himself up en his powerless battered body with his enough reserved energy scraping a hurried flight sticking his okapi into Ngwatus big neck as in steek hom doodstil, Ngwatu who rebelled against principles of the nzuzos empire ubhodile on the spot the next event commenced, Tayi-G flexing his muscles waiting impatiently for the charming pretty biza skull he even tried theatrics like a seasoned Mohammed Ali wanna bee Sviwe closed his eyes in the process of the event leading to this match fight but knowing that there was no way out he braved on, the crowd in support of their future king, for Sviwe to preserve his good looks the best form was to attack. Titus wanted to slaughter Sviwe with an okapi in his bloodstained hand a black hanky lone figure stepped into the ring, the black Italiano from lahlu'mlenze as an intruder Titus abandoned his okapi midair the black hanky stranger saved Sviwe but to the rest of zanas crowd he ruined their grand finale.., Rasta the big man carried the pretty biza Sviwe on his shoulder like a sack of maize meal-meal from the grinder.., Titus raised his hands in victory like he had just knocked out Mike Tyson during his heydays.., pretty biza Sviwe was taken to lahlu'mlenze to recuperate otherwise Rasta the big man enjoyed to being the black Italianos apprentice for years, Rasta had a father by the name of Moyana, Moyana had been bras with the black Italiano since they were of the same age en these chomies in their younger days had been instrumental in the formation of skwata style that planned to oust bra zakes en with the plan failing they had to form their own lahlu'mlenze

1.7   the black Italiano knew he was nurturing a potential future threat, the slender youngster en his chomie Mandilakhe were from the market where they left auntie Mavis she did not bother them about checking on her every half an hour on their way home from the market they met Welani going back home earlier from esigele he says to the youngster malankane en his brazana Mandi, the is a funeral gathering lana sigeleza khona at school when malankane ask Welani some more questions he did not open his mouth ever again the youngster malankane in his own funny creative phrase once more he says how can you expect them to know about such fateful so feared ritual which every swane and poole.., every man and women has to go through, the slender youngster malankane en his chomie rushed to the funeral gathering at school, when they arrive they saw people sitting on the school chairs listening to an old white bearded chap speech behind the pulpit, the landlord king bra zakes took his turn en went to the pulpit, people clapping hands slender malankane says bra zakes likes to be known as the one who encourages people to speak in vernacular along the way he falls in the trap of speaking foreign en says isingesi niyasiva mos.., the youngster says from that remark then bra zakes makes a unity call to them zanas people of emapozana to work together as one suggesting that the was loose ends en that some people were trying to be ungovernable.., to malankane he seems to be an autie who does not know the difference between a funeral procession en the disciplinary room, he says that we darkies have to work together for things to be right again, bra zakes then again goes on to say.., clouds that are dark someway brings new beginning en old ways are gone.., the slender youngster malankane says bra zakes is like a politician that uses every opportunity available to endorse their own business.., he then stepped down, then a man dressed in all white took his turn en slowed himself to the pulpit, he was the black Italiano dressed in all white en he says is hard for him to swallow the words that say is a brand new start when somebody lost his or her life, the youngster malankane recognizes him once more as a scoundrel from lahlu'mlenze trying to be a saint in emapozana swindling the young prince declaring war against nzuzos is a blunder the youngster malankane says king zakes the landlord had been humiliated en attacked in front of his subjects, his sons had to control their tempers as it was unheard of what black Italiano had done.., the landlord king mzaka-zaka listened on like he was not on the receiving end as the man sarcastically threw his shoes on him, the black Italiano fooled the youngster malankane dressed in all white he thought he was a black master who will never change, Mandilakhe the youngsters chomie will brag that he knew it was the Italiano darkie from the word go.., everyone knew all stories about the man in all white tales of how police would call him when they wanted to grill en pin him down on suspicious mind.., the black Italiano would tell cops to bring him fried chicken en all those up there take - away, after eating he would ask for a permission to go to the toilet they agree en grant him permission to go, they will wait for hours on end en he was gone he will send cops a call back message when they return his call he informs them of his intended destination en he says they should talk about catching him if they can the slender youngster malankane says thinking that black Italiano had no where to sleep the previous night makes him feel that he had a hand in a cause of the funeral gathering.., en calculating bastards for sure the cops them gatas that is will want to know his where about the night before Nomsa died, again he took out his white hanky from his back pocket en wiped perspiration only discernible to himself off his shiny forehead, if he lands in a danyane cell he will be doing Rasta the big man a feva, before the slender youngster closed his eyes en fall asleep for the third time, the black Italiano dressed in all white spoke again

1.8 he says that all he want to tell them is not to let the matter lay to rest,where he comes from they hunt every mthakathi down.., with that he gracefully went back to his chair. the youngster malankane feels sorry for mama ka nomsa who passed away en that he is bleeding for nomsa en other children who are physically en mentally ill treated en pledges that he will hunt the bastard who did that to a poor girl. malankane says he does not care even if he is faced with bra zakes en the black Italiano because his loyalty ends when harmony of nature is tampered with Nkosinathi remembered this month no one on behalf of the oulady had come to do errand for her Titus the one in charge wanted justice done, the duty of caring out the mandate of the state rested with Titus the first prince.., having a look at the five register document that kept all the protection fee records, money floated in cyberspace, when counted there was a shortage the contrasting ink on the oulady page checking the accounts her slot in the book is unsigned the amount has been entered with different ink en when the mula is counted it does not balance Titus tells Nko, that they are supposed to do something, if other.., mamparas hear that they are sleeping en not taking action they will take advantage of the nzuzo brothers Titus listened as Nkosinathi shows him two different pen colours on the protection fee balance register, Titus appeared bitter about his father bringing new ladies in their lives almost daily the new vrou selling stuff at the market coming home late at night these days.., en that is why the nzuzo brothers are having slip-ups in the protection fee balance register en the different handwriting is his, the nzuzo brothers decided that they have to punish her for trying to cheat them.., en that she made them think that she had skipped the country in order to cover-up for her protection fee crimes, Titus the first prince sealed the fate of the traitor.., the nzuzo brothers on a witch hunt went past mancanes spaza shop to buy some matches.., the slender youngster malankane when he parted ways with his chomie mandilakhe he did not go home he took a turnaround en headed for kwandengezi a new tavern on the boundary separating lahlu'mlenze en emapozana.., ou tymas like Dengezi are glad to see laatie- tjies interested in literature, especially rare African literature which malankane saw Dengezi reading en die ntwana malankane vra hom om te se.., what was he reading..,why is he reading the book onderste bo. Dengezi did not answer malankane the second question immediately Dengezi the magpie was paging a book with the cover picture of Nelson Mandela Dengezi started to relate the stories of the man on the cover picture to the youngster malankane he says you see ntwana it's a pity you are not familiar to this world renowned figure, Dengezi was associating the world figure life stories with the da vincis code as one en the same thing when the youngster wanted to make him aware that his tummy is rumbling out of hunger
for a while Dengezi the magpie at a click of his fingers, he beckoned his young shabby looking girl en instructed her to make a kota with slice of a polony for malankane en after munching a kota for the third time he stepped out of the Dengezis mansion tavern on his way home not even afraid of the dark night, the slender youngster malankane claiming that the Almighty is his paragon..,He grants him water of life (not the golden bottled one) He adeptly star treks the slender youngster malankane through the shacks of zana. where the slender youngster malankane shack is, its far from kwandengezis tavern, so he, had to walk a bit, from a distant he saw some smoke baptize the atmosphere, as he drew nearer, its as if the shack is on fire.., indeed his own makhulus shack was on fire

1.9 everybody rushed around some carried water buckets en lazy ones worried about their prized possessions, flames gulped down the shack in no time, it took the zanas water efforts to beat the evil flames, the youngsters brazana mandilakhe rushed over to see if he was fine he also reminded the youngster that the nzuzo brothers wanted what belongs to them, the youngster controlled himself from getting angry, he wanted to know how the fire started, from auntie Mavis, she told the youngster she smelt some smoke in the kitchen, the flame was switched off there was nothing on the stove, she says she checked everything was off, she went back to sleep only to be woken by the next door neighbours telling her that the mkhukhu was on fire, there after auntie Mavis told the youngster to make a plan cause she wanted to sleep, slender malankane took auntie Mavis to former pretty bizas shack which was now in the hands of a man who calls himself bhaka-bhaka ezimnyama ngekani.., the man opened himself to auntie Mavis who says to the man they don't have a place to sleep he says who said he does not like visitors ntwana looking at the youngster malankane trying to make it look like he did not want to be seen as in favour of auntie Mavis the youngster malankane says women can getaway with murder for beauty enshrined in their bodies is welcoming prospect to all, he says if it was him alone he would have not opened the door but then he would have told him that this is former pretty bizas shack.., the slender youngsters brazana mandilakhe came around on a Saturday morning, he even brought something for them to eat.., en suggesting that they go to his makhulus shack to see if everything was gone, the youngster could see in a newspaper article with a subheading warning residents to pay their protection fees in time en that was a proof enough to the youngster that this was the work of the nzuzo brothers they are the ones who burnt his ou magrizas shack for his failure to pay the protection fee in time Nozizwe enjoyed being bra Zakes Nzuzo the landlord king of emapozanas first lady, en rumours has it that the queens children that she raised for the landlord king were not his, as the slender youngster says in his own words.., the world would be strange if things were normal en normal when things are strange.., the landlord bra Zakes neglected Nozizwe en entertained other women in the name of nation building, no one could tell the landlord king what to do, the day his first born son turned ten, she was never seen or heard of in emapozana ever again, he became mad cause he no longer had some one to treat like a dog.., the sweet sound of the noisy sirens which winded our ears up signaled the entrance of the stapiya vans in grand style, four of the cops vans in a total, the former pretty biza Svidge had allied with the law enforcers as he had led them to Etwatwa the official royal residency as, from what the slender youngster heard their landlord king is a shark, as for small prawns he casts them to the for ever hungry princes en the stapiya that is cops in their four vans came by with the charmer pretty biza Svidge to raid the landlord king bra Zakes Nzunzo en the Nzuzo brothers.., the slender youngsters chomie Mandilakhe from their hiding spot he pointed to the other autie in blue next to the charmer pretty biza Sviwe with bandages en stuff the slender youngster malankane says if he was not mistaken that's a mjita who took auntie Mavis golden wrist watch, he had no clue that he was an undercover stapiya he says he was completely driekopstaan the slender youngster malankane says in his mind the chances of getting back his golden wrist watch went down in flames.., again the slender youngster malankane says in his own words by the look of things this is the end of the Nzuzos dynasty, Mabhulus vision proved to be infallible a waar for real.

TWO REVIEWS
by Mphutlane Wa Bofelo

Izinhlungu Zomphefumulo (Emotional Pain)
Bongekile Mbanjwa

Publisher: *Botsotso*

"Izinhlungu Zomphefumulo" (Emotional Pain) is a ground-breaking, bi-lingual triumph. Bongekile Mbanjwa's aptly titled collection of IsiZulu poems - whose English meaning is rendered by fellow poet, Siphiwe ka Ngwenya - is both the individual, anguished cry of a tormented soul as well as a reflection on the psycho-physical damage of cultural emasculation, moral degeneration and socio-economic injustice that is still present in post-apartheid South Africa. As such, the poet puts as much emphasis on the ravages of personal traumatic experience as on social decay which destroys self-identity and self-worthiness:

Ubumina buyangigqilaza	*My real self is enslaving me*
Ubumina bungiphendule uhlanya	*My real self is turning me into a mad person*
Ubumina bungivalele ekhoneni	*My real self has locked me into a corner*
Ubumina bungibophe izandla nezinyawo	*My real self has tied my hands and legs*
Ngihambe ngiqholosha	*I swagger when I walk*
Ngibuye ngikhwantshe umsila okwenja	*And came back with my tail between the legs like a dog*

Beneath the rhetorical question "how can you blame me?" there is a sense of self-blame, resignation and hopelessness: "we have tried \ the struggle is over\ deep waters are quiet\ let us give up."

Several poems deal with the theme of the encroachment of Western civilization on African Culture in the form of culturally irrelevant laws and socio-political arrangements. These have led to the disintegration of traditional African norms and value systems and undermined the family and other key social structures. In poem after poem the poet associates the past with the authority of morality and culture and the present with social decay and the decline of values:

Yayimilelendlu kaZulu	*The house of Zulu was standing*
Wawungafunga uthi yinqanawe uqobo	*You could swear that it was a ship*
Kepha namhlanjeiwise okwebunga	*But now it has fallen*
Ngibheka emuva ngibone ukukhanya	*I look back and see light*
Ngibheke phambili ngithole	*I look forward and get*
Inkungu ivimbanisele	*A mist clouding*

The dichotomy between traditional\rural and modern\urban is also captured in photo-images of a cow, a man clad in ipheshu, a young woman in traditional attire and a sprawling township juxtaposed against pictures of a car, a young man clad in denim jeans and shirts and dark sunglasses, a young lady in a mini-skirt and sky-scraping flats. While Mbanjwa is a social worker and expresses affinities with the poor and marginalised in most of her poems, ironically, some suggest that she shares the view that children and offenders have been granted excessive rights in the new dispensation.

In the poem **Iqolo**, the child-support grant, which many researchers have indicated has played a tremendous role in rolling back poverty, is accused of making "all beauty disappear". Despite researches showing that a lot of the money from the child support grant and other social grants is used by families to address basic needs, the poem refers to the child grant as a big fire, and asserts that through the grant the government is hitting the community with a slap with a back hand. The negative attitude towards the grant is informed by the perception that young people deliberately fall pregnant to be able to qualify for the grant, leading to unprotected sex, which works against the "ABC" message of the campaign against HIV\AIDS:" *"The youth is crying for a child grant\ you spoke about the condom\ you will regret it\ the majority say, "if I could have so many babies I would be rich"*

In the poem, **Kufana Nokufa (It is Similar to Death)**, the emotional pain suffered by a victim of jilted love is likened with death: "*it brings shame \ it brings hatred\ and brings anger \ confusing the mind\ and life vanishes.*" The poet recalls the romantic moment of meeting with Prince Charming and the ecstatic experience of falling in love:"*I pronounced love\ you welcomed me with affection\ you gave me real self\ and covered me with jubilation \ I sweat from happiness.*" She contrasts this with the bitter ending, as she and her beloved got estranged:"*I struggled like a frog \ things got worse\ you fumed with anger\ I got angry as if drenched by water*". Though the reasons for the fallout are not mentioned, the sub-text seems to portray the poet as the victim.The imagery employed to pour out her bleeding heart evokes feelings of emptiness, a sense of worthlessness, a sort of dying: "*I am a bed of wishes\ I am a pillow of pain\ I am a blanket of questions \ Endless questions.*"

Indeed, rhetorical questions are the main device used to highlight a sense of hopelessness, directionlessness and a lack of clarity of vision:

Ngifikelwa wumbuzo ongapheli	An endless question comes
Singama kanjani isihlahla	How does a tree stand
Ngaphandle kwezimpande na?	Without its roots?
Ukukhula kukhona singanakekelwanga?	How can it grow without it being nurtured?
Umthunzi wokuphumula UZulu wona?	What about shade where Zulu will rest?
Angisayikhulumi eyokuthela izithelo	I don't even mention bearing fruit

Endless questions resurface when the poet pours out her soul regarding the myriad challenges and problems bedevilling our country: " crime is taking another step\ how many corpses are going to lie down\ how many drugs are going to enter our country\ how many are going to shake the hand of HIV\AIDS\ South Africa are you silent?"

The social worker voice of Mbanjwa - who has worked at the KZN Society for the Blind and is currently working for Epilepsy South Africa - comes out in poems such as **Ukuze Ukuqonde (For You to Understand)**. This poem is an emphatic take on disability, and chastises patronising and paternalistic attitude towards disabled people, forcefully appealing to readers to put themselves in the position of those living with disability:

Ukuba umbele wemali	To be a breast of money
Wezikhungo zabakhubazekile	For those who are abled
Uphinde ubeyibhange	And be the belt
Lezisebenzi zikahulumeni	For civil servants
Ubuye ube ucansi lezinyawo	And be a grass mat for feet
Izinyawo zeziqumama	The feet of the rich
Sezifinya ngendololwane	The feet of the wealthy
Ukuze ukuqonde	For you to understand
Yiba nokukhubazeka	You must have a disability
Ucele usizo ubusuku nemini	And ask for help day and night
Akukho namunye osabelayo	No one will listen
Kuhulemeni nasemiphalatini	The government and the community
Bonke bayaqinsekisa	They all emphasize
Baqinisekis'ukungabaluleki kwakho	They emphasize your worthlessness
Kwawena uzizwe ungelutho	And you also feel worthless
Kodwa ukuze ukuqonde	But for you to understand
Yiba nokukhubazeka	You must have a disability

Mbanjwa does not stop at recording and articulating pain and suffering. In poems such as **Yima Kancane (Hold On), Silapha Ukuzohlala (We are here to stay)** and **Ziqhenye (Be Proud of Yourself),** she preaches hope and tries to inspire the disabled and marginalised of the world to believe in themselves and to assert themselves in an environment that seeks to contain and limit their possibilities: "Live your life like others/ Enter where others enter / arrive where others arrive / I say, be proud of yourself".

Though Siphiwe ka Ngwenya has tried his best to make the English version of the poems as close as possible to the meaning conveyed in IsiZulu, to feel the beauty of the language and the spirit of the poems it is useful for one to hear them being read in isiZulu. There is no doubt this effort by Mbanjwa and Botsotso will go a long way in pushing forward the agenda of the promotion and preservation of indigenous languages of Azania\ South Africa.

a mountain is an upside down valley
by Shabbir Banoobhai

Publisher: *Shabbir Banoobhai*

Like most of Shabbir Banoobhai's recent works, "a mountain is an upside down valley" consists of prose and poetry that is reflective in nature, betraying an intensive process of meditating, and an inquisitive raising of questions about the nature and essence of things visible and invisible to human eyes. It investigates the essential meanings of concepts and values such as love, compassion, justice and knowing God. While the very act of engaging in such serious and critical reflections is a bold exercise, it is much a bolder act to actually share with the rest of humanity one's deepest feelings, emotions, thoughts, and imaginations.

The very act of Shabbir Banoobhai opening up not only to his immediate family but also to the rest of the world, selflessly sharing with all humanity his inner life, is an expression of love and faith in humanity. This is indeed an act of subduing the self to the one and only real purpose of our being on earth…..knowing the Ultimate Truth. Through deep reflection, Banoobhai seem to have arrived at the point where what he sees in human beings and the rest of creation is that everything is a reflection of the light of God. Even in the darker and darkest side of humanity and other creatures Banoobhai sees a flicker of the primordial and transcendental light: "Jealousy is awe without generosity; injustice, remembrance without forgetfulness"

How is this possible? I find the answer to this in the assertion of Sheikh Muzaffar (of the Helveti Sufi order) that the purpose of remembrance of the Creator (Zikr) is to make us graduate from seeing with the eyes of the head to seeing with the eyes of the heart. Sheikh Muzaffar says: "If you can see through your heart you will know all men, all things, you will see like a telescope with wide lens. If you see only with the eyes of the head you are not different from an animal. An animal has a head, eyes, nose, muscle, skin, ears; you are alike, except that you can see through your heart's eyes. When you see with your heart's eyes, all space opens for you"

This collection of prose and poetry makes me want to believe that it is complete devotion to immersing the self in remembrance of the Creator and an unflinching quest for His or Her face that allows Shabbir Banoobhai to see a valley in a mountain and to behold veiled light in darkness. What runs like a thread through this book, and indeed in all Banoobhai's work, is that looking within allows us to discover buried treasures and to therefore be able to live fully in each moment but be able to see beyond the moment, so that we are not tempted or deluded by the life of living for the moment. "A mountain is an upside-down valley" shows us that seeing beyond form, tasting the essence of life, being in touch with the reality beyond the moment, is possible only when we grasp the reality that everything is invisible and that it is only through such awareness that everything becomes visible.

Real awareness is moving beyond the knowledge and sight of something to being in something and ultimately to becoming something. In this and other works Banoobhai presents the view that God is love and love is Godly. Loving is seeing God. Knowing God is being in love. Being in love is being in God. It is not enough to know about love\ God. Real knowledge is seeing the love of God in everything, being overwhelmed and consumed by that love, being in that love and ultimately becoming that love.

If you read "A mountain is an upside down valley" seriously, with the eyes of the heart, you will see that it is the creation of a person who has arrived at a point where he has become a living expression of that love himself.

All the Days
by Robert Berold

Publisher: *Deep South*
Reviewer: *Vonani Bila*

Finnish correspondent Mark Waller gives me Robert Berold's latest poetry collection, All the Days whilst having breakfast in my apartment in Polokwane. "He mentions you in the poem **Journey**". I giggle. I've seen this poem before in New Coin magazine and loved the strong imagery in the following lines:

> *Hillbrow. Wanderers Street.*
> *Taxi-blasted chickens stand in cages.*
> *I was born here. Florence Nightingale Hospital.*
> *It used to be a dreamy flatland of pensioners and nurses.*
> *The city filled and emptied every day as orchestrated by the law.*

My fiancée Gudani grabs the well-designed slim volume of 70 pages excitedly, and the breakfast of jungle oats will get cold, a waste – but she seems to have found rich nourishment in Berold's narratives. She goes through the long poem **Journey**, competing with our 18 months old son Mhlahlandlela who demands to be breastfed whilst pretending he's literate. After an hour or so, this woman who seldom reads poetry tells me she's gone through the entire collection and concedes the poems are penetrable. Her favourite poem is, "**To my room**". Here, Berold sings about his deepest love for books. It's also a quest to recreate a warm world, and be recreated by the knowledge that he draws from books and life's observations within and outside the walls of his room.

> *When I moved here you were much darker,*
> *so I put in windows and the aerial bookshelf*
> *that runs around above head height. Now*
> *I sleep with a weight of books above me.*
> *I want to cover them, like birds, to keep them quiet.*
>
> *I've slept three thousand nights in your arms.*
> *You have absorbed my snoring and my dreams.*

"His poems are accessible and relate to everyday life. I can read the book over and over like a good novel," Gudani says. Then I grab the book and I, too, discover that Berold is calm, frank and unpretentious, his language lucid, although sometimes his tone is wild and rough. Still, in the nakedness of poetry in which he bears his feelings open, he is not defenseless. His controlled simple yet intense lines and strong imagery have the ability to reach out to non-poetry readership.

In his letter to Irish poet Yeats, the Indian poet Rabindranath Tagore writes: "When passion does not come from deep sensitivity, it becomes just a series of well-crafted words. Then it has to make up for its lack of candour and inner assurance with exaggeration; since it cannot be natural, it resorts to artifice in order to prove its originality". Berold's poetry is original and responds directly and candidly to life. Its goal is not just self-expression; it is an expression of his soul. All the Days is a tapestry of the poet's life at 60, and the refreshing poetry is layered with lyricism and explores space, language, place, spirituality, transition and above all, love that the author cherishes. Here, the poet sees with his heart and not just the eyeballs. Berold wrote this collection over a period nine years in different parts of South Africa, including during his one year stay in China where he was teaching English.

Letter to Mary is a tribute to an incredible black woman from Sepanaphudi in Limpopo who was a domestic worker at the Berold's. Rob Berold cannot hide his intimate love for this woman who saved his life by nourishing him in a healthy and loving way. "It was this realization, rather than any political conviction, that drove me from the white career path and into working with rural black people," Berold says.

> Long ago you carried me from the noise into the sunlight.
> How much I've tried to pay my debt to you.
> Only to find that debts of guilt are endless.
> And debts of love? There are no debts of love.

What I've always struggled to understand with the white people who were raised up is how they came to loath these black maids who wiped away their soiled nappies when their parents were consolidating the gains of apartheid. Berold is surely humane and a different sort of white.

Letter to Mary is juxtaposed with **Visit to my mother**, whose pink and red Impatiens in her garden look artificial. "But all of Rosebank and its malls look artificial to me" because, "her racism is savage as ever", but "I've come to see her because she's been ill. In intensive care. She could have died", he writes, giving the reader space to reflect on their upbringing and the type of mothers they've had. Berold's mother is 86 years old and appears convinced that blacks are just interested in sex and stealing.

> "The Sunday Times has a black editor, hasn't it?"
> ...."That's why it's full of sex", she says.
>
> ..."that's all they're interested in – sex and thieving."
>
> ...'They all pinch", she says.

This frank conversation between son and mother is real and handled calmly. The son deplores his mother's racist habits. But, yes, like we say in Xitsonga, vele ra manana a ri na xilondza [a mother's breast bears no wound], she remains the mother. What is pleasing is that at the end of the poem the mother apologises for being a bad parent, and the son accepts the apology, hopefully not grudgingly.

Berold's careful and unfaltering eye has granted him insight into both black and white territories. Over the years, he worked in rural development throughout the country, setting up handcrafts cooperatives and encouraging small-scale sustainable farming. The poem **What I hated** deals with the seeming catharsis that generally characterizes the white community in post-apartheid South Africa irrespective of ideological inclination. Just as the Truth and Reconciliation Commission found half-measured truths, and failed dismally to rebuild the lives of victims of political violence, it'll take greater efforts to get the verkrampte and liberal beneficiaries of apartheid to confess that their whiteness accorded them some benefits. A few years ago, Adriaan Vlok, a former minister during the apartheid regime, washed Frank Chikane's feet as a biblical gesture of reconciliation. But very few people followed his act. Berold's poem seems to suggest that in order to rebuild this land, even the radical white left whose devotion to the liberation struggle and human rights was beyond measure have to deal with the sins of their forefathers. And the question lingers, should the white community take full responsibility for the apartheid crimes as once suggested by the ill-fated Carl Niehaus in what he termed the 'collective guilt of the white community?'

Vigilantly observing the ways of the apartheiders from the sidelines, Berold hated "the way they spoke about beating up kaffirs", and surely, blacks were beaten and dehumanized in barbaric ways. Blacks were killed; some disappeared mysteriously; some were dumped in mass graves; some souls are still in Vlakplaas; many blacks still live in shacks and are landless. But "what had kaffirs ever done to them or me?" He asks soul-searchingly, "and if I wasn't part of them; what was I part of?' I guess Berold is part of a set of caring poets whose generosity of spirit and sheer honesty cannot be contained in one simple ideology.

The poems included in All the Days are constructs from an open heart yearning for unconditional love, dignity and seeking the truth. Berold is a man aware of his past and approaching old age. One of my favourite lighthearted narratives is My Bakkie, Berold's brand new Toyota Hilux 2.0 which he bought in 1984 – the same year he published his first book of poems. This is the car he's driven over 300,000 km to Cape Town, Durban, Johannesburg and Skukuza. But, now it's a skorokoro. "One summer evening I came back with the groceries and parked on the slope outside my house. As I switched on the kettle I saw my bakkie rolling down the hill. I shouted to it "Hey! Where the fuck you going? But it didn't listen, just carried on rolling over the veld, demolishing a fence post, crashing slowly into one of the big logs anchoring the nursery."

The theme of death permeates several layers of Berold's poetic imagination. In this collection, My Death, describes his death wish.

> I want to die in bed or sitting on a chair –
> like an old car when its axle engine gearbox
> all stop working simultaneously
>
> Here's my will signed and witnessed –
> forget about a coffin, use a plank
> put me in the ground and plant a celtis tree.

It's interesting that artists and poets alike often express how they wish to die and how their funeral proceedings should be directed. Sculptor Samson Mudzunga has carved a wooden coffin for his burial. He performs death rituals by sacred Lake Fundudzi in the former Venda. Novelist Es'kia Mphahlele wished that his poetry be read out loud and followed by echoes of drums at his funeral. He wanted to be wrapped in a cowhide, cheap but meaningful as Berold's preferred plain plank. At Mphahlele's funeral in Lebowakgomo, instead of poetry rendition, the mourners sang Christian hymns and read the Bible. They followed their acquired tradition planted by the missionaries. Speaker-after-speaker talked about Mphahlele's vast land of letters, but couldn't even pluck a verse from his books. Instead of a cowhide, they stuffed his remains into an expensive casket. Do they feel guilty? I doubt it. Berold's other poems that explore death, changes, spirituality and eternity include *The Water Running, The Valley, Does it end, Letter to Mary* and *The Fire*.

I have many favourite poems in the collection but the more reflective, simple poems, intense and layered with humour, brevity and sheer honesty like **The fire, the book of changes, at the wavelength of earth, All the days, To myself at 20** and **Journey**, are the most effective and carry with them the immediacy of impact.

Finally to note that the playful child in Berold hasn't seized up, so he composed a sound poem called **Two cats**:

> Kattekung kattebong
> kattekung kattebong
> ke-kattekung ke-kattebong
> kattebong kung.

THREE REVIEWS
by Frank Meintjies Of Deep South Publications

The Hurricurrant.
Rosamund Stanford

Rosamund (Mindy) Stanford's poetry is distinctive: her words are carefully chosen and she tends to break down experiences & objects into small particles. Her poems are partially set in the Eastern Cape where she currently resides, something we learn from the cover note.

However, Eastern Capers will not see in her poetry many signs of that part of the world. This is partly because her poems are focused on interior spaces and the personal; she also opts for the micro rather than the wider view. This is less the case with her poems set in KZN; they give a better sense of place. In this sense her poems engage in different ways.

Stanford's poems seem to be wilfully un-rhythmic. She does not allow her poems to settle into a rhythm; it's almost as if she wants the reader to be aware of a certain discomfort and unease in the inner life. Is this what is meant when she refers to her poems as unruly lines? Or does this lack of rhythm point to the particular mood of the author? We are tempted to make such links between the poems and her life, especially as we are informed that the author has retreated to her rural location.

In one of her poems she says, "no one is here/in this pit of a grey ribbed valley/ hulk of a stony ark/ and I've waited so long down here/ hunkered like a frog when hooves passed/ in the night of night." This poem, **Hooves**, gives a good sense of the poet's style. The naming of the poem tricks you: the poem is less about hooves and more about cowering and bracing in response to un-named fears and pressures. When reading Stanford's work the idea is to be mindful of false clues and to steer clear of quick conclusions.

Another finely crafted poem is 'Forefathers'. It again shows the meticulousness with which she lays down words, creating a complex pattern that does not easily give up their meaning. However, when you have worked through the clever wordplay and the layered imagery, there are rich pickings.

The poem **Pa's passing** is a particular milestone. It is powerfully touching and one of the more direct. Noting that … "we stand still, like sleeping horses/in awe/before our mourning" the poem speaks compellingly about loss. It also captures in effective ways a love for, and closeness with, the farm. It refers to time and to familiar things on the farm that create both counterpoint and a sounding board for deep inner feelings.

Malikhanye
by Mxolisi Nyezwa

Mxolisi Nyezwa's small collection is sharp and quirky and filled with engaging reflections. Some poets give away little of their essence, but in this case the poems give a strong sense of the man. His work is shot through with a sense of place and his positioning within it. This is established in the first poem in which he declares "I live in the city/near the violent sea" and in the fifth poem where he says "I live in a township". In his poem **From a blue container** he simultaneously alludes to the shipping container among the shacks that is his workplace and, in a deft expressionist turn, to the sky, earth and sea. The container represents his feet on the ground, but through artistic ability he is able to turn his gaze outward to the ocean and upward to the sky. These parts of nature communicated their own form, but also reflect his reality and mood. In this connection, it is not so much the sea, but life on shore that is beset by violence.

Nyezwa's poems constantly grapple with the toughness of life in the townships. The "children without food" and the anguish of people around him crop up repeatedly. On the one hand, the adverse and persistent socio–economic conditions are part of context and setting as he explores other themes; on the other hand , the poet unambiguously conveys that such conditions are intolerable and unacceptable, even shocking.

In this work, Nyezwa plays with existential questions. These questions lift the book to a different plane. It is the openness with which he discusses his searching for answers and meaning which captivates and engages the reader. After referring to "a black room with two gigantic stars" and "the storms in my life", he asks: "what happened? / what really happened?/ what did I really see?" Although he cannot understand "why a man exists", one gets the sense that some information, some understanding and some light is trying to break through the clouds. As he puts it, he sees "someone is whispering … something is written … someone is saying something."

Nyezwa often refers to being alone and to living alone. Linked to this lonesomeness, he reveals certain difficulties in his relationship with women. One poem suggests he is fleeing from any real interaction, almost crying out that he is not ready for it. At the same time, the poet wants to love again. He wants to know someone who, as he puts it, is "like a place of colours/of pastels/that rise from the canvas/ in glory and confusion".

In looking to regain the capacity for love, the poet notes:

> I must follow
> the direction of the wind
> I must feel my way
> around this heart of mine

The third section of the book is devoted to a father's anguished love for a child, a child that died all too soon. The extended poem, **Malikhanye,** is beautifully written, where the writer uses his pen for a deep engagement with the child who has gone. In this way he is processing his deep loss. Even though he ends the poem with the words "I want to know how the sea flows …. Why things have to happen like this", it is possible that, through writing of this poem, he arrives at a deeper understanding - or at least, a plateau of acceptance.

The work of Nyezwa, already an award winning author, stands out because of the imagery he uses. The phrases and images he crafts are taken from the depths of creativity. His work is not an easy read – in only a few cases do the poems have an easy-to-access narrative line. But there is much to be gained in the wholeness of each poem, in following the threads that run through the collection and by simply immersing oneself in the lushness of Nyezwa's figurative language.

Light and After
by Kobus Moolman

Moolman has set out to structure this work in a deliberate way. A single closing poem aside, the collection is arranged like a sandwich. There are two smaller sections at either end and a more substantial middle one called 'Light'.

The two outer sections are highly defined. In the first, called 'Home', Moolman writes about his house and about his relationship with the house. In **Window**, a man contemplates a window "that refuses to look at him" and "that treats him like a non-entity". Another poem **The Room** works with the tightness of space that is in the house. At some point he even pulls the sky into this cramped space. The poem ends with reference to a man "with the whole world collapsing on his head" and of a sky "that echoes like a man on a narrow bed".

In the last section, all the poems are named after body parts. This poet's acumen is on display, as is his capacity for calm but intensive reflection even as he contemplates the world through the body. Thus the hand "swim (ming) through the day" is startled when someone walks past and "gasps and swallows short breaths/when anyone asks it a question". The foot calls the other foot "stupid" and "small". And the shoulder is, for the writer, a repository of ongoing and incredible pain.

The middle section is slightly more fluid; it also breaks out from the confines of rooms and body into wider space. Overall though, this section is a consideration of nature and a probing of feeling through nature. The 'Light' is about the light (and the dark) as it plays on mountains, trees, the bay view and stones. The poems convey a sense of solitude but not a restless isolation. It seems the poet is comfortable with wallowing in a contemplation of nature and its soft echo in his feelings. For most of the poems in this section, the 'observing' human being appears to be at the edges of what is happening. **Boy**, a poem of great strength, is an exception. In it Moolman writes:

He looks at the world
and is frightened

by the size of what
his hands will become

Will his dream
ever fit into such an old space

Already he can feel
the pinch of the sky

Already the light is too small
for his new wing

If only Moolman had more pieces such as this in the book. His focus on the solitary person communing with nature gives a consistency to his collection, but I would have preferred it - if only for the sake of diversity - if he had brought more about people, about relationships and more of himself onto the pages.

Despite my concern about the narrowness of the preoccupations, 'Light and after" remains a tasty sandwich confirming Moolman's status as an award winning poet. Here is mastery over the tools of poetry: the skilful but disciplined play with words; the deftly chosen images; the re-imagining of familiar things to stimulate fresh perception; the smalls twists that spark emotional connections.

Submissions

Submissions to Botsotso magazine & website

All submissions are welcome. Please send original, unpublished work in any South African language and be careful to keep a copy as we cannot be held responsible for loss or damage to manuscripts and cannot return work.

Simultaneous submission of the same work to several magazines/publishers is not acceptable. However, should you wish to withdraw work from Botsotso kindly inform us timeously. All work received is considered by the editorial board but due to the high volume of work received we are not always able to respond to each contributor. As such please bear with us if you do not receive feedback!

No payment for published work is offered as our budget is very limited but selected work will qualify you for a complimentary copy of the magazine. Copyright of all published material remains with the writer/artist but the proceeds from the sale of Botsotso magazine are used for new projects. As a non-profit entity we are struggling to achieve financial self-sufficiency – a very difficult goal to achieve as the "market" for new, original South African writing (especially for poetry and short fiction) is extremely small.

Please remember to include your contact details: name, postal and email address, telephone number.

Botsotso magazine appears irregularly as a number of important variables have to be satisfied – quality and diversity of submissions, funding, time to edit – but we do attempt to produce at least one edition a year. Some work is included in both the electronic and hard copy versions of Botsotso but we reserve the right to publish in one or the other as circumstances change.

Botsotso Publishing
Box 30952, Braamfontein, 2017
or
botsotso@artslink.co.za

BOTSOTSO TITLES

Literary Journal

BOTSOTSO – *poetry, fiction, essays, photography, graphics/drawings*

Numbers 1 – 16

Poetry Collections

WE JIVE LIKE THIS	**Botsotso Jesters** *Siphiwe ka Ngwenya, Isabella Motadinyane, Allan Kolski Horwitz, Ike Mboneni Muila, Anna Varney*
NO FREE SLEEPING	*Donald Parenzee, Vonani wa ka Bila, Alan Finlay*
DIRTY WASHING	**Botsotso Jesters**
5	*Clinton du Plessis, Kobus Moolman, Gillian Schutte, Mphutlane wa Bofelo, Lionel Murcott*
GOVA	*Ike Mboneni Muila*
GREETINGS EMSAWAWA	**Botsotso Jesters**
ISIS X	**Editor:** *Allan Kolski Horwitz Elsbeth e, Sumeera Dawood, Lisemelo Tlale, Makhosazana Xaba, Elizabeth Trew, Myesha Jenkins, Arja Salafranca, Baitse Mokiti, Riana Wiechers, Bongekile Mbanjwa, Anna Varney*
SOULFIRE EXPERIENCE	*Siphiwe ka Ngwenya*
SAVING WATER	*Allan Kolski Horwitz*
A PRIVATE PART	*Lionel Murcott*
FALLING FROM SLEEP	*Mark Espin*
BELLA	*Isabella Motadinyane*
POETIC LICENCE	*Mike Alfred*
MMA AFRIKA (*Poems in Sepedi*)	*Tlou Setumu*
IZINHLUNGU ZOMPHEFUMULO (*Poems in IsiZulu*)	*Bongekile Mbanjwa*
(EMOTIONAL PAIN) English translations:	*Siphiwe ka Ngwenya*
VIEW FROM AN ESCALATOR	*Liesl Jobson*
BLUESOLOGY & BOFELOSOPHY	*Mphutlane Wa Bofelo*
SECTIONS OF SIX	**Editor:** *Allan Kolski Horwitz Natalie Railoun, Matodzi Ramashia, Alison Green, Abu Bakr Solomons, Khanyi Magubane, Thuto Mako*

Poetry CDs

PURPLE LIGHT MIRROR IN THE MUD

Botsotso Jesters (Allan Kolski Horwitz, Isabella Motadinyane, Siphiwe ka Ngwenya, Ike Mboneni Muila, Anna Varney) and Lionel Murcott
Soundscapes: James de Villiers

ROOTS AND BRANCHES

Yoliswa Mogale, Allan Kolski Horwitz, Mark Espin, Mphutlane wa Bofelo, Myesha Jenkins, Siphiwe ka Ngwenya, Chantal-Fleur Sandjon, Khanyi Magubane, Ike Mboneni Muila, Lesley Perkes, Lionel Murcott, Phillippa Yaa de Villiers; Soundscapes: James de Villiers

Short Fiction

UNITY IN FLIGHT

Maropodi Mapalakanye, Peter Rule, Zachariah Rapola, Michael Vines, Phaswane Mpe, Allan Kolski Horwitz

UN/COMMON GROUND — *Allan Kolski Horwitz*
POST-TRAUMATIC Anthology featuring 22 writers — *Editor: Chris van Wyk*
JAIL BIRDS AND OTHERS — *Muthal Naidoo*
CANDIDATE AND TOTEM / SING, BABYLON — *Marcelle du Toit*
100 PAPERS — *Liesl Jobson*
OUT OF THE WRECKAGE — *Allan Kolski Horwitz*

Drama

BLIND VOICES Four plays for radio — *Kobus Moolman*
IKASI AND OTHER PLAYS — *Gha-Makhulu Diniso*
KUYANUKA AND OTHER PLAYS — *Gha-Makhulu Diniso*
THE PUMP ROOM — *Allan Kolski Horwitz*

Art

MANUSCRIPT EXHIBITION 2000 — *Curated by Anna Varney*
MANUSCRIPT EXHIBITION 2002 — *Curated by Anna Varney*

Childrens Literature

BLUE WINGS

Text: Allan Kolski Horwitz
Illustrations: Anna Varney

Co-Productions

COMEBACK

Peter Esterhuysen and Paul Mason (with Bodhi Books)

EMZANA SHACK COLLECTIONS — *L. Sojini (with Pole, Pole Press)*
DONGA — *Editor: Alan Finlay and Paul Wessels (with Bleksem and Dyehard Press)*